Practical Boat Building For Amateurs
Full Instructions For Designing and Building Punts, Skiffs, Canoes, Sailing Boats,

by Adrian Neison

with an introduction by Roger Chambers

This work contains material that was originally published in 1900.

This publication is within the Public Domain.

This edition is reprinted for educational purposes
and in accordance with all applicable Federal Laws.

Introduction Copyright 2018 by Roger Chambers

Self Reliance Books

Get more historic titles on animal and stock breeding, gardening and old fashioned skills by visiting us at:

http://selfreliancebooks.blogspot.com/

Introduction

I am pleased to present another book in the "Boat" series.

The work is in the Public Domain and is re-printed here in accordance with Federal Laws.

As with all reprinted books of this age that are intended to perfectly reproduce the original edition, considerable pains and effort had to be undertaken to correct fading and sometimes outright damage to existing proofs of this title. At times, this task is quite monumental, requiring an almost total "rebuilding" of some pages from digital proofs of multiple copies. Despite this, imperfections still sometimes exist in the final proof and may detract from the visual appearance of the text.

I hope you enjoy reading this book as much as I enjoyed making it available to readers again.

With Regards,

Roger Chambers

PREFACE TO THE SECOND EDITION.

The fact that a second edition of "Practical Boat Building" has been called for is incontestable evidence that the title Mr. Neison gave to his work was an appropriate one; nevertheless, as no work is so perfect that it cannot be improved, it was considered possible to render the second edition of Mr. Neison's treatise even more practically useful than the first. With this end in view, as Mr. Neison was travelling in America, Mr. Dixon Kemp undertook the revision of the book, and, whilst retaining generally the original text, has amplified it or altered it where necessary.

The sections relating to designing and clench-work building have been entirely re-written, and the instruction given on these matters is now in accordance with the most approved methods followed in this country.

CONTENTS.

CHAP.	PAGE
I.—Introductory—Designing	1
II.—Tools and Materials	19
III.—Punts	35
IV.—Clench-Built Skiffs	49
V.—The Rob Roy Canoe	75
VI.—The Sailing Boat	85
VII.—Canadian Bateau—Canvas Canoe—American Shooting Punt	98
Index	107

Practical Boat Building for Amateurs.

CHAPTER I.

INTRODUCTORY—DESIGNING.

THE skill necessary to build a boat of some form which will be serviceable and pleasurable is possessed by few amateurs, and as boats and canoes are now so extensively used in athletic and other amusements, and the followers of the rod and gun find them almost indispensable in certain varieties of these pursuits, no doubt very many amateurs would like a little information which would assist them to construct such things. The reason, perhaps, why amateurs do not more often try their skill on boat-building is because there are technical difficulties which seem to throw a barrier in the way of all who do not care, or have not the time, to spend on a thorough study of the subject. Such an idea is a mistake, for boat-building is well worth the amateur's attention; for it is really a simple craft, not requiring nearly so much skill and technical knowledge as good joiner's work. For instance, anyone who can make a box or a table would be able to make an ordinary punt. Of course, to construct a light punt which would row well would require more skill than this, for it would embrace an amount of technical knowledge not generally possessed by the amateur.

Everyone is aware that boat-building, in some form or other, is practised all over the world, by savage as well as by civilised nations—the inhabitants of the former often showing as great skill as the best artisans and mechanics of the latter nations. For instance, the war canoes of New Zealand and the prahs of the Malays equal in every respect the skill displayed in the large sailing and rowing craft of Europe, while the Canadian birch bark canoe and Esquimaux ryah or skin canoe, of which our Rob Roys are a reproduction, show an amount of ingenuity and skill of construction which is unsurpassed. When such facts are considered, it is surprising that more attempts to develop the useful art of boat building are not made in our home workshops; for surely, with the better materials and tools at our command, and the ample resources of pen and pencil contributed so largely from all parts of the world by various authors, the amateur, with the exercise of a little patience and study, should be able to make for himself a presentable and useful craft.

To be able to build a boat well, and to his own ideas and plans, requires that the amateur should be both a designer and builder, which, in their turn require that he should be an efficient draughtsman and carpenter. No one can hope to succeed in building a boat to his own plan, unless he is fully able to design and lay down the lines and body plan of the proposed craft, and added to this in many kinds of boats, such as a small sailing boat, or a steam launch, it is necessary that he should be able to calculate the displacement and the position of the centre of buoyancy. With this knowledge at his command, an unlimited field is opened to the amateur boat-builder, as he will be able to build after his own ideas. Many must have experienced the difficulties of getting some peculiarity in design carried out for them by a boat builder whose knowledge, being generally of the rule-of-thumb type, finds it difficult to understand any innovation that may be put before him; but the amateur designer who has mastered the theory of naval design, and who is capable of performing the calculations referred to, can dictate with confidence to the builder. But it is not everyone who has the leisure or inclination to master the substance of works on naval design, such as "Yacht Designing," and yet have ideas of his own on small boats to which he would like to give effect.

But putting aside theoretical design, the building of very light canoes and skiffs intended to be used under peculiar circumstances, can advantageously be undertaken by one's self, as many little ideas of fitting and arrangement which in ordinary cases would not be carried out on account of the expense attendant on them, can be made and tried, and, if found to answer, adopted.

Generally the boats suitable for an amateur to build are those which do not require such a display of skill as is shown by the professional builder; but even these, which we may call the higher class of boats, are not beyond the amateur's reach if he will give the subject the necessary attention; but most are in too great a hurry to finish their job, or are too fond of trying to make things "do," so that they destroy the harmony of the whole structure by want of care in small particulars. No one can hope to be successful when he works on a want of system; but, nevertheless, it is the rock upon which very many maiden efforts at boat-building are wrecked. The amateur will always find it worth his while to be careful in his work; he cannot afford to try and imitate the *apparent* haphazard decision of a professional builder, who has acquired the knowledge of what *will* do only by years of apprenticeship, which the amateur hopes to do without. A very little error in the first steps of building a boat will throw out all the planking, so that they cannot be made to fit properly into position. If the ordinary amateur can make a skiff or canoe from the instructions contained in these chapters he will have no cause to complain; but he should not attempt any of the lighter description of craft at first.

The simplest boat that an amateur can build is an ordinary punt with square ends, such as one sees on rivers for fishing purposes; but this can be developed, if he likes, into a more complex craft, very light and very small, drawing very little water, and capable of going anywhere and everywhere. These are sometimes made to be propelled with a scull or a light pole, and are intended to be pushed through a bank of reeds or "wriggled" over a mud bank in pursuit of wildfowl. Sometimes they are made to take to pieces and pack up into a small compass; but such a punt requires more skill to construct.

A punt is a useful craft, generally very safe and reliable, and often the source of a great deal of pleasure. We should advise the amateur, if he is a good carpenter, to try his skill upon a lighter punt than an ordinary fishing punt, which requires more tools than the others in the shape of clamps; and besides, the lighter craft is the more useful.

In the choice of skiffs it is not so easy to decide, because there are so very many varieties and patterns useful for different purposes, and then again, skiffs are built in so very many different ways. Those long, narrow, and shallow craft, weighing but a hundredweight or so, require the perfection of a workman's skill, especially when built with planks or battens, running the whole length of the boat. Few boat-builders even are possessed of sufficient knowledge to build them. Perhaps the most useful craft is a short broad boat, fairly easy to row, and capable of carrying a little sail in rough water. Such a boat is suitable for fishing or shooting, and will carry a small picnic party. A light sharp craft, pointed at both ends to carry one, or two at a pinch, is also a handy thing to anyone living on a river or lake, who does not canoe. The latter requires neater workmanship, the former presents the greater technical difficulties in shaping and fitting it together.

In canoe building no decided pattern can be laid down, because nearly every canoeist has his own idea; but it may be taken as a general maxim that all canoes are difficult to build, chiefly because they have to be very light, and yet exceedingly strong. A Rob Roy canoe is the simplest except a flat-bottomed shooting canoe. Ringleaders and sailing canoes—such as the Nautilus and Pearl—are all more complicated, especially those with centre boards. Some sailing canoes are really nothing else than miniature yachts, and are provided with so many different fittings for their working and safety that it requires a great deal of judgment and knowledge to build one. Neat and careful fitting together are the principal requirements in canoe-building, and as most of the material can be bought ready dressed to size, but few and inexpensive tools are required.

A small sailing boat comes well within the reach of an amateur's skill, and, in many respects, it is an easier kind of craft to construct than any other, except a punt; for in building carvel-built boats neatness of fitting is not so essential, as all the interstices and gaps are filled up and made watertight with pitch and oakum. The material used, however, is of heavier dimensions, so that more and a greater variety of tools are required. If the craft is to be of a large size, it is necessary to bring some knowledge of naval architecture to bear on it, as a little error in the amount and disposition of the displacement may make a great difference in the sailing powers of the boat.

The same may be said of a small steam launch, except that in this case a greater knowledge of engineering is required, as the lines must be designed with some regard to the power and weight of the machinery and speed intended to be attained.

Mention has been made of drawing working designs for boats. It is not to be expected that any amateur will go through a course of mechanical drawing simply that he may be able to draw the lines of his proposed craft, but he will find it a great advantage to learn sufficient to enable him to draw the cross sections and water lines correctly. In doing this, a few instruments are required, but these have no need to be expensive. If, however, the amateur wishes to produce such drawings as may be seen in a naval architect's office, he must obtain a complete set of instruments. This all amateurs are advised to do, if they can afford it, and they will in return find much amusement and plenty of opportunity for study and research in the highly interesting study of naval architecture.* The instruments he will require, and must have, are a two-foot rule, divided to one-eighth and one-sixteenth of an inch. Scales 2in. to the foot, 1in. to the foot, $\frac{1}{2}$in. to the foot, $\frac{1}{4}$in. to the foot; a straight-edge, 2ft. or 4ft. long; a pair of 6in. dividers; a 6in. set square; a set of pear-shaped curves (see Fig. 1), and three or four French curves of the patterns shown in Fig. 2 (these must

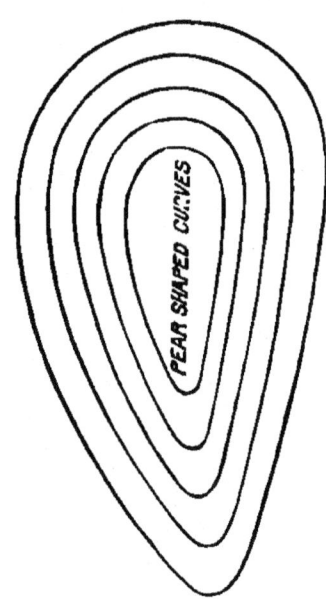

FIG. 1. PEAR-SHAPED CURVES.

---

* The books most likely to be of service to the amateur designer are "Yacht Designing," and "Yacht and Boat Sailing," published at the *Field* Office, as these contain all the necessary calculations and the lines of many well-known yachts, boats, and canoes of all sizes.

be at least 6in. long, but a larger—say 9in.—size would be better). There are usually eight pear-shaped curves to a set; the largest 1ft. by 7in., and the smallest 3½in. by 1½in. An H drawing pencil, indiarubber, and half a dozen drawing pins. To draw the water lines the amateur will also require two or three long red pine or lancewood penning battens, two or three short and very thin battens (called splines by naval architects), and half a dozen or more lead weights (see Fig. 3) to hold them in position. In Fig. 3 these weights are clearly shown. They consist of a block of lead about 5in. long by 1½in. wide, by 1½in. deep, as seen in

FIG. 2. FRENCH CURVES.

A   B   C

FIG. 3. LEAD WEIGHTS.

A, B, and C. These lead blocks are mounted on a piece of hard wood, which tapers to a point, as shown in the figure A, which acts as a sole to the lead blocks. This had best be hard wood, such as mahogany; it must be about a quarter of an inch thick. The point of this wood rests upon the batten and holds it in position when in use. Any amateur can make these for a few shillings, while he cannot buy them for less than six shillings apiece. The red pine or lancewood battens may be bought at any mathematical instrument makers from about 1s. each.* They vary in pattern and length from 18in. to 60in. long. Fig. 4 explains the use of the battens; in this drawing the batten, *a a a*, is shown held in position by the lead weights *b b b b*, for one of the water line curves, but usually all the weights are kept on the one side only of the batten, otherwise the weights would obstruct the continuous penning of the curve.

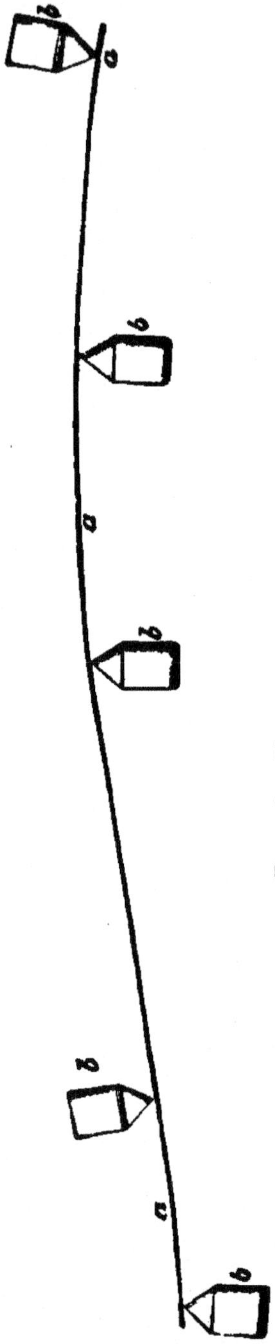

The body plan can be made either by the pear-shaped curves or by the thin spline battens. Besides these things the amateur will also require the use of a large flat board or table on which to pin down his paper while making his drawing. For paper the amateur must procure a sheet of

FIG. 4. PENNING BATTEN AND WEIGHTS.

---

* All the instruments, battens, curves, scales, &c., can be obtained of Mr. Stanley, Great Turnstile, Holborn, who supplies the Admiralty.

DESIGNING.

Imperial cartridge paper, or, what is better, continuous cartridge paper; or, for strength, continuous mounted plan paper.

To make the drawings of his boat the amateur must proceed as follows: He must first determine the scale he intends to make his drawing on; if possible, he should not make it less than about 2ft. long, that is to say, for a boat 12ft. in length, use a 2in. scale, for one 24ft. use an inch scale. The ¼in. scale will be useful for the sail plan. In pinning the sheet of paper down to the table, try to get it flat and smooth, or otherwise the lines may not be true, and the paper soon gets dirty.

First draw the line, L.W.L. (see Fig. 5), to represent the load water line in the Sheer Plan. This line must be drawn so that there will be room above for the gunwale sheer, and beneath for the draught of water and Half-breadth Plan. Next determine the length of the load water line, and mark it off, as at A B. It will be convenient now, by the aid of a square, to draw a perpendicular at A and B (see T F and U O).

The breadth of the boat we will assume has been determined to be 5ft. This distance must be marked off on the L.W.L. at C and D for the Body Plan, and perpendiculars drawn. A perpendicular will also be drawn at the mid-distance, E; this will represent the middle vertical line of the body plan.

The line F G will now be drawn for the base of the Half-breadth Plan; this line will in reality be the middle fore and aft line of the boat. It should be drawn so far below L.W.L. as to allow ample room for the draught of water and extreme half-breadth.

A line, H I, will now be drawn in the Sheer Plan to represent the *top* side of the keel. The depth of this line below the L.W.L. will be decided according to the draught of water to the top of keel; in this case we will assume it to be 6in. Another line, J K, will be drawn underneath H I to represent the depth of the keel,

10 PRACTICAL BOAT BUILDING.

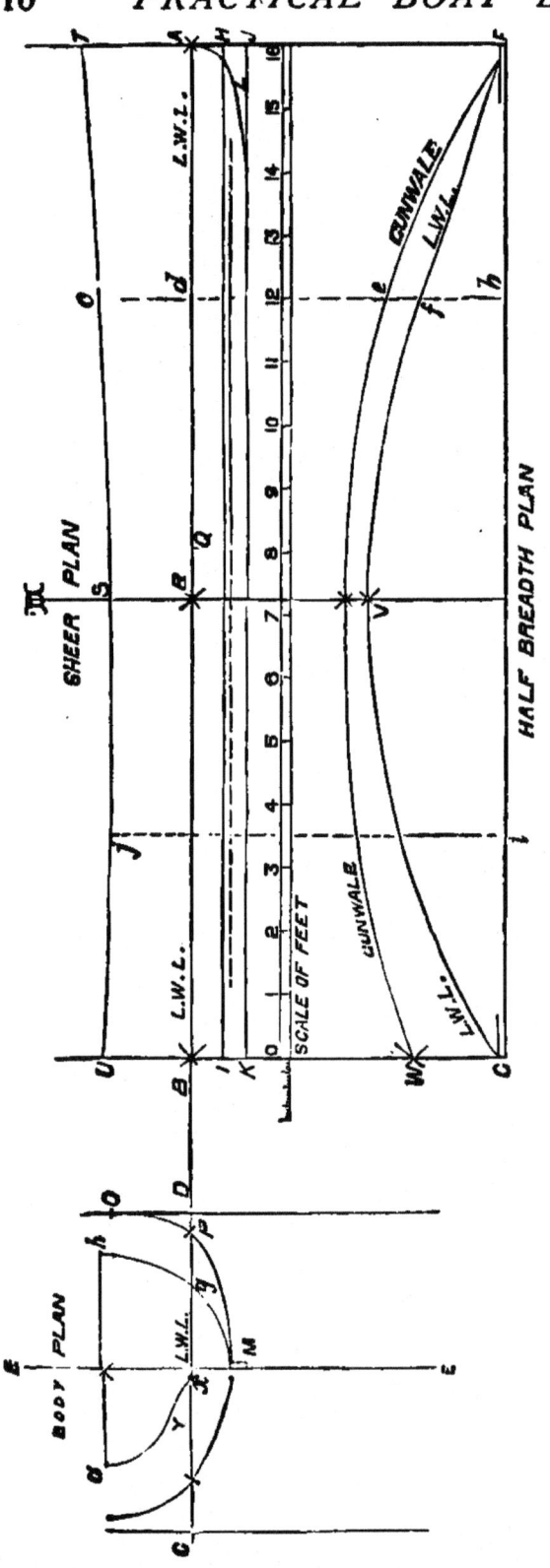

Fig. 5. Body, Sheer, and Half-breadth Plan of Boat.

assumed in this case to be 3½in. With the small end of one of the pear-shaped curves of suitable size the rounding-up of the fore foot can now be drawn as at L. It will be observed that the keel has been drawn parallel to the load water line, and the draught of water would therefore be equal throughout. This is by no means an arbitrary condition, and for a sailing boat it might be necessary to commence a gradual rounding up towards the fore foot from amidships, or the keel might rake upwards from the sternpost.

The dotted line immediately under

the L.W.L. represents the direction that the *lower* edge of the rabbet line will take. It allows ½in. of keel to be inside (for back rabbet) and ½in. for thickness of plank. Thus it is 1in. below the top side of the keel.

The midship section will now be drawn. First draw the line M to represent the *half* thickness of the keel on E. The whole thickness will be 2½in., so the half thickness will be 1¼in. This part of the keel must be drawn at a distance below the L.W.L. to represent the exact draught of water amidships.

The form of the midship section will now have to be determined. We will assume that the craft is to be easy and light to row yet have a pretty flat floor. The greatest beam will be nearly at the gunwale, and the breadth at the L.W.L. will be 6in. or 8in. less than the greatest breadth of 5ft. Only *half* the section need be drawn. The section will be in form something like that shown by M, P, O.

If the scale be no larger than 1in. to the foot the curves of the section will be drawn by aid of one of the pear-shaped curves, but if a much larger scale be used the small thin spline battens and weights can be used to draw the curve by.

A distance representing the distance the rabbet line is below the L.W.L. must be marked off on M on the right hand side of the middle line of the Body Plan. This will, of course, represent the point where the midship section joins the keel.

A good height amidship for such a boat will be 1ft. 4in. Mark off this distance above the L.W.L., on the perpendicular, at D as at O. Next set off 4in. from D towards P on L.W.L. The rabbet mark on M, the point P, and a point about 4in. below O, will enable the draughtsman to sweep in the curves of the midship section. Take one of the small pear-shaped curves that will cover these points, and run a pencil round the curve. If a pear curve cannot be found to take in the three spots, the line must be drawn in two or more pieces, unless a spline can be got round the curve.

The position of the midship section in the boat will have now to be determined. The section is generally placed a little abaft amidships, and ·05 (or $\frac{1}{20}$) of the length of the load-line abaft the *middle of the length*, as set-off at Q (Sheer Plan). One-twentieth of 16ft. will be, as nearly as possible, 9in., and this distance will be set-off from Q to R. A perpendicular will be drawn here right through to the base line, F G of the Half-breadth Plan. The height of the midship section must now be taken from the Body Plan (D O) and transferred to the perpendicular at R. The height was 1ft. 4in., and mark this off for a point in the sheer from R to S.

A good sheer for the fore part of the boat will be ½in. to the foot. The length of the fore part or fore body is nearly 9ft., therefore the amount of sheer from S to the stem will be 4½in. This, added to the height (1ft. 4in.) amidships, will make 1ft. 8½in. Set off 1ft. 8½in. on the fore perpendicular (A to T) above the L.W.L. *This will represent the height of the top of the gunwale at the stem.*

The sheer for the after part will be ¼in. to the foot. The length of the after body is a little more than 7ft., and the sheer can be taken as 1¾in. Add this to 1ft. 4in. (the height at S), and the distance is 1ft. 5¾in. Set this off above the L.W.L. on the perpendicular B to U. *This will represent the height to the top of the gunwale at the transom.*

Now take a stiff batten and place it on the spots U S T, and fix it by the lead weights; humour the batten so as to get a fair curve, and use other weights at frequent intervals to secure it whilst sweeping in the curve with the pencil.

The load water line curve must now be put in on the Half-breadth Plan. Take the distance from P to the perpendicular E on the body plan, to represent the half-breadth of the load water line at the midship section. Set off the distance on the perpendicular in the Half-breadth Plan from the base line to V. (The base line is, of course, the line F G). Take a thin batten and place it on the spot V, and bend it round to F and G, securing the batten at intervals by lead weights. The load line should retain its greatest breadth (nearly) for some distance on each right and left of V; this will give what builders call a good "straight of breadth." The line can be given an inch or so hollow approaching F forward, but will be kept convex approaching G aft. The *half* thickness of the stem should be drawn at F; the half thickness will be 1in.; and the *half* thickness of the sternpost should be drawn at G; the half thickness here will also be 1in.

The gunwale line will now be put in on the Half-breadth Plan. Set off the full half-breadth outside V—in this case 2ft. 6in. Next the half-breadth at the transom must be decided upon. The breadth of the transom is generally a little more than *half* the full breadth amidships—in this case we will take it to be 2ft. 10in.; so the half-breadth will be 1ft. 5in.; this distance will be set off on the perpendicular from G to W.

The batten must now be taken again and fixed by a weight on the spot above V. It will then be curved aft to W. The breadth will contract very gradually at first, as shown, and then more suddenly near W. Forward the curve will be full, so as to make good roomy bows.

The transom will next be put in. Take the half-breadth (G W), and set it off on the Body Plan to the left of E at the height U B (taken from the Sheer Plan). This half-breadth is represented by a dotted line projecting at right angles from E. Next set off the *half* thickness of the stern post at *x*. Take one of the small pear curves and draw the curved line from *a* to *v*, where there is an inflection. The pear curve will now be reversed, and the part of the transom from *x* to *y* completed. Other sections can be now put in. A convenient place for one will be 4ft. from the stem or F at the point represented by the dotted line *b c*, running from the Half-breadth Plan and Sheer Plan. To get the section into the body plan, take off the gunwale half-breadth *b e*, and place it to the *right* of E at the height *c d* above the L.W.L. (from the Sheer Plan). The dotted line (*h*) to the right of E in the Body Plan represents the gunwale half-breadth. Next take the half-breadth on the L.W. (Half-breadth Plan) from *b* to *f*, and transfer it to the Body Plan from the perpendicular or middle line E to *g*. The section will join the keel M at the rabbet line. A small batten or pear-curve from the rabbet mark through *g* to *h* will enable the draughtsman to draw the section.

An exactly similar process will be followed to get in the section at *i j* (see Sheer and Half-breadth Plans).

Other sections can now be put in at convenient intervals, and then other water lines below the L.W.L.

To fair the drawing above the L.W.L., a line should be drawn on the body plan across the sections, midway between O D. The half-breadths taken from the sections on this line must be set off at their proper stations in the Half-breadth Plan, and a curve drawn, by aid of a batten, similar to the gunwale curve, &c.

In putting in the sections it will in practice be found convenient to have them at equal intervals, but it is by no means essential that they should be so.

In the drawing the stem above water is represented as vertical.

Of course the stem might be curved as the fancy dictated, and the transom and sternpost might be raked.

After the drawing is made by pencil it can be inked in with Indian ink, by aid of a bow pen, and the battens. Water lines are usually drawn in blue ink.

In designing a boat it is necessary that some attention should be paid to the position of its centre of gravity and buoyancy. In general language, the centre of gravity may be said to be that point on which the boat would balance equally, supposing it to be suspended. The centre of buoyancy is the centre of the hole which is made by the boat displacing the water when she is floating. The centre of buoyancy is *always* in the same vertical as the centre of gravity, and in designing a boat care must be exercised so that when it has a full load the position of the centre of gravity may not alter materially from its position when the boat is floating empty; otherwise the trim of the boat will be altered, and she will be either down by the head or by the stern.

Of course in all small boats it is impossible to keep it steady, as the load varies so much, but as far as it can reasonably be done, it should.

A canoe is the easiest so to arrange, as the chief load, which is the occupant, does not alter its position very much. The common sense of everyone must tell him that the centre of gravity alters with every change of position of the occupant of the boat.

Of course a boat floats better and is propelled easier when the centre of gravity is in or about the greatest midship section, as the lines of a boat are generally designed with this end in view. Practical small boat-builders do not trouble themselves much about these things, as they acquire a certain "rule-of-thumb" knowledge, gained by long and varied experience, which tells them that it is all right; but the amateur has not this experience to guide him. A rough and ready but sufficiently accurate way to find the centre of buoyancy of any small boat, the water lines having been drawn, is to reproduce them in wood as a half model.

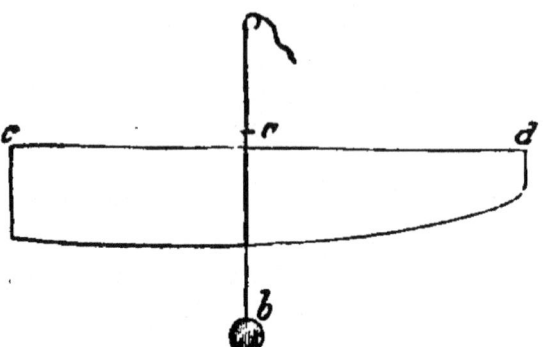

Fig. 6. Model.

Pieces of clean pine will be used of the exact thickness of the space between the water lines. The shape of the water lines (half-breadth only) will be traced on both sides of these pieces of pine, and the edges pared down to the lines. They will be then screwed together and smoothed off down to the edges formed by the traced lines. To find the centre of buoyancy, suspend the model in a horizontal position by a screw at *a* (see Fig. 6), hang a plumb line *b* from the screw, and mark where the plumb line cuts the model. This line will show the fore and aft position of the centre of buoyancy, which is the more important position to know.

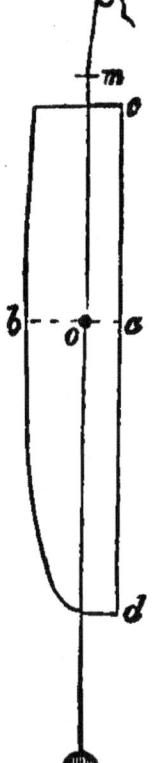

The vertical position of the centre can be thus found: Suspend the model as before, but by the stern end (see *m* Fig. 7), until the plumb line is exactly parallel with *c d*. At the point *o*, where the plumb line cuts *a b*, will be the vertical position of the centre of buoyancy.

Fig. 7. Model. Of course the screw *m* in Fig. 7 must be shifted until the upper side or load line of the model, *c d*, is in an exactly horizontal position; and the screw *m* in Fig. 7 must be shifted until the plumb line is exactly parallel to *c d*. Only the *under water* part of the boat will be used for this experiment.

The position of the centre of lateral resistance can be determined in the same manner by cutting out of a thin piece of pine a section to represent the *under water* portion of the Sheer Plan.

The area in square feet of a boat's load water line, roughly, is the breadth on the load water line multiplied by the length, and again, multiplied by the fraction 0·7, termed co-efficient. Or the area will be about three-quarters of the product of the length and breadth (taken as stated) multiplied together.

The total displacement or weight of the boat when floating at any load line will be her length and breadth on the load line multiplied together, and again multiplied by the existing or proposed immersed depth amidships to *rabbet of keel*; the product again multiplied by the fraction 0·3 (termed co-efficient) will give the bulk of immersed body of the boat in cubic feet or fractions of a cubic foot. Divided by 35, the weight of the boat in tons or fractions of a ton. (35 cubic feet of salt water go to a ton, and 36 cubic feet of fresh water.) The sum will be as follows:—

Length L.W.L.	16ft.
Breadth L.W.L. ×	4ft.
	64
Depth ×	0·5ft.
	32·0
Co-efficient ×	0·3
	9·60 cubic feet.

This reduced to tons will be:

```
35 ) 9·60 ( ·27 ton, or about 5¼cwt.
     70
     ---
     260
     245
     ---
      15
```

Acting on the directions given in this chapter, an amateur, otherwise ignorant of boat-building, should be able to design a boat for himself. Practical experience in the use of boats is, however, necessary to enable the designer to form some idea of the proper proportions and materials to be used; a thorough and reliable knowledge of these, however, can only be acquired after careful study of different kinds of boats, an insight into some of which will be given further on.

The amateur should not despise the suggestions thrown out on the advisability of acquiring a theoretical knowledge of boat design, as nothing conduces more readily to success than a thorough knowledge of a craft in all its branches.

CHAPTER II.

TOOLS AND MATERIALS.

In this chapter the tools, implements, and materials that are required for boat building will be considered, and their respective uses pointed out. Some of those that will be mentioned are not absolutely necessary, the amateur being able to dispense with many which the professional builder requires. This is especially the case in the implements used, because the amateur will often be able to make shift with some little contrivance which would, though answering the purpose, delay the professional too much, so that it is better worth his while to have a suitable arrangement provided.

In the first place the tools required to build a boat are not very many or very expensive, though some of the expensive sorts may be used with advantage in the finer and lighter built boats and canoes. Supposing that the amateur intends to turn his whole attention for the time being to boat building, intending to build several, he will require more tools than if he only intended to construct one. On these conditions the following will be required. For saws he will require a rather coarse rip saw of say six teeth to the inch, for sawing off strips for stringers and some kinds of ribs; he will also want a panel saw, which had better be rather fine. Besides these two saws, two others are very useful, especially in building light boats, but they can be dispensed with, these are a small tenon saw and a compass saw. Let the compass saw have rather fine teeth, say eight to the inch, as it will be required mostly on hard wood. All these should be sharp and bright, because, as they are much used, the labour would otherwise be excessive. In sawing teak and very gummy pine, it will be necessary to chalk the saw when using it, otherwise it drags heavily in the cut. In the matter of planes, a jack and smoothing plane are required, and if possible a rebate plane, or "rabbet" plane, and a pair of match planes. These are required for dressing square rabbets, and for tongueing and grooving the planking in the deck or lockers. These latter are best made with the tongue rather long, so that a little channel about one-sixteenth or one-eighth of an inch wide is left, which is afterwards caulked. Mortising and other chisels of one inch, three-quarter inch, one-half inch, and one-quarter inch in width are wanted for mortising in the stem and stern posts, and cutting the rabbets in the keel and stem and stern, if a plane is not used. A one inch and one-half inch rather flat gouge are very useful in making a paddle or an oar, but to finish these nicely without too much labour a round sole plane is wanted. Spokeshaves and draw-knives, which are nearly related to planes, are both used in boat building. They are both needed on the oars or paddles, and on the seats and rounding of the fore foot, row-locks, &c. Chisels having been mentioned, the amateur will hardly need to be reminded that a mallet is also necessary, and, besides this, a moderately heavy carpenter's hammer and a light hammer, of about 4oz. or 6oz., are wanted; the last is for light canoes and clinching the rooves of the boat. A few gimlets and also some fine bradawls and augers are wanted, these last being of a size which is suitable to the nails used, that is, just a little smaller, so that the nail makes a nice fit. The boat-builder also requires a brace and set of bits, and of these those known as American auger bits are the best. Those bits which must be provided are one inch, three-quarter inch, one-half inch, three-eighth inch, and one-quarter inch auger bits, and also centre bits to correspond in size; besides these, some fine gimlet bits, a driver bit, a large and a small rose bit, a counter sunk for metal, and a ditto broach. All these are very useful, more especially in large boats, principally those which are carvel built. In small canoes and skiffs the brace and all its appurtenances are not required, though they are very handy in mortising the keel for the stem and stern. A light bench axe and adze are of great assistance in building a heavy boat, as with its aid the keel, stem and stern posts, bilge keels, and any trusses or the timbers, if any, in the counter, are quickly dubbed down to size; a large hammer, and a small hammer, spirit level, rooving iron, pincers, auger, steel square, vice, and compasses, will also be required. To this already lengthy list must be added a 2ft. or 4ft. rule, which is best in 12in. joints, and a square and a bevel are required. A few light wrought iron clamps (wooden ones are not so easy to handle, though they are much lighter) for holding the planking in position while being nailed, are very handy and useful.

In addition to these tools, several implements or accessories are necessary; and in building large and heavy boats, where heavy wood is required in the planking and the ribs, these are especially required, and the more so when they are so stout as to require to be steamed and bent into shape, all of which require that proper provision to do it shall be provided.

The first and most necessary are the trestles or stocks upon which the boat is built. These are required for making every class of boat or canoe, and their duty is to raise the work off the ground to a convenient height to operate on, and also to provide a firm basis to build from. It is to these that the keel of the boat is secured to make it steady while building, but in heavy or carvel built boats the keel is raised off the ground on blocks of wood. The stocks must be firmly and strongly made, the best shape being shown in the sketch (Fig. 8). The horizontal piece on which the keel rests should be a 3in. deal.

Having got the stocks, the next most important adjunct is the frame, or model, on which the boat is to be built. These are made in different ways, but they all consist of a set of frames, either three or five joined together, so as to be very firm and steady. These frames give the form to the boat, and act as a temporary set of ribs, holding the planking in its proper position while being nailed together, to be removed as soon as the boat has been made sufficiently stiff. Sometimes,

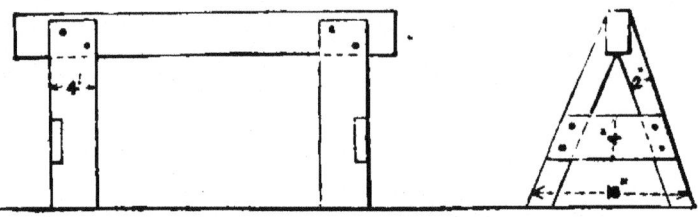

Fig. 8. Trestle Stocks.

generally in small skiffs and canoes, this frame is dispensed with, the keel, and stem and stern posts, with the help of a light template at the midships, doing duty for it. This arrangement requires more knowledge to use, because, as there is no gauge between midships and the ends of the boat, it is quite possible to flatten one side of it more than the other, and unless the amateur exercises the greatest care he will do so. To avoid this error, it is of importance that the planking for each side of the boat shall be cut in duplicates so that they are exactly the same in length. If one side of a boat is made a little flatter, it affects the steering, and makes the boat unsteady, besides preventing it floating on a straight keel. Some boat-builders make the frames for their boats very neatly and carefully, and arrange them so that the moulds, which represent the section of the boat

MOULDS. 23

can be adjusted closer or farther apart, so as to be capable of doing duty for very many different sized boats, the lengths of course, only differing, the widths remaining the same. These moulds are fac-similes of the cross sections of the boat to be built as are produced in the drawing of its design, as is shown in Fig. 5. In Fig. 9 the moulds of the midship section and forebody of a boat are shown, and from this an idea of how to make them can be formed. They are made of one inch or one-half

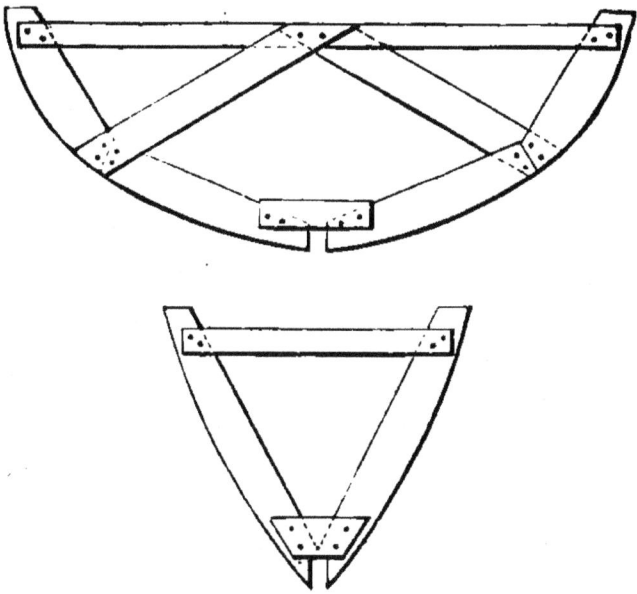

FIG. 9.   MIDSHIP AND FORE BODY MOULDS.

inch wood, according to their size, and are neatly nailed together with braces, so that they cannot alter in shape. The load water line should be distinctly marked on each, or, better still, a small bar of wood should be nailed across each mould at the load water line. A more detailed description of using them will be given farther on.

To make the moulds, the drawing must be laid off full size on the floor by the aid of pine or American elm battens. These battens will be of various sizes, from $\frac{1}{2}$in. for body plan to $1\frac{1}{2}$in.

for sheer of gunwale. They will be kept to the curves by sharp pointed nails driven into the floor on each side of the battens.

Last of all may be mentioned the kiln or apparatus for steaming wood, to facilitate its bending to the shape of the boat, an accessory of very great utility in heavy boats. This apparatus consists of a boiler and furnace to make steam, and a large tray in which the wood which is to be steamed is placed, after which it is filled with steam from the boiler. A kiln such as is usually constructed by amateurs and small boat builders is a very primitive affair, being generally a makeshift, but in the case of large building yards, expensive plant, in the shape of boilers to carry steam at a high pressure, and strongly made wrought iron chambers to receive the wood to be bent, is put down.

In making a kiln the only portion which requires care and outlay is that which is to be used to raise the steam in, and in which the steam acts on the wood. As the furnace can be contrived in many ways, perhaps the simplest and cheapest boiler that can be got is an iron pot boiler, such as is used in a washhouse; the arrangement being simple and inexpensive, it is well suited to an amateur. With the following description and sketch, anyone should be able to make one for himself. A boiler 15in. to 18in. in diameter should be obtained, the larger the better. This must be set in a small furnace made by arranging some bricks on the ground in the form of a parallelogram, as shown in Fig. 10, leaving one end open as shown, which make the mouth of the furnace. This must be provided with a piece of sheet iron as a door, and by judicious manipulation of this a good draught can be maintained. At the opposite end a small chimney must be built. The brickwork had better be mortared together, but if only required for a short time common clay will answer. In this brick furnace the boiler must be set so as to leave about twelve inches between it and the ground. This arrangement is

STEAM KILNS.

clearly shown in Fig. 10. An inspection of the figure will show that this plan allows the flame full play on all the sides and bottom of the boiler, the boiler being suspended by the flange

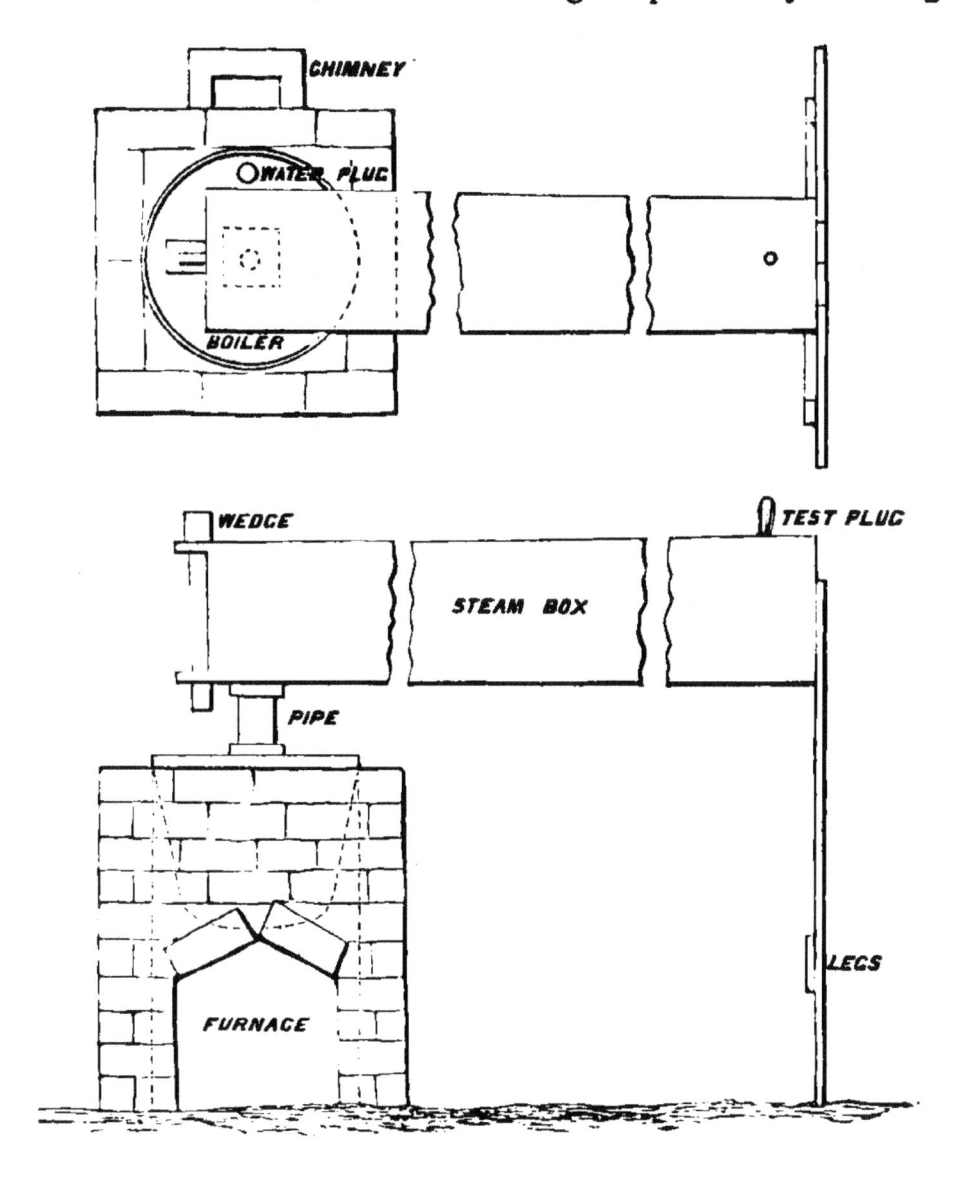

FIG. 10. KILN FOR STEAMING WOOD.

which is always made round its rim. The boiler must now be fitted with a good strong lid, so as to close it all in. This lid may be made of one inch pine, put together with screws, and had best be made of two thicknesses, placed so that the joints cross each other. It must be just the size of the boiler and flange, and fit well, so that, with the addition of some red lead and stout string neatly laid round the boiler flange, it will be fairly steam tight under low pressures. This lid is in no way fastened to the boiler, it retaining its position simply from the weight upon it due to the steam box, as will be hereafter described. It must not be expected that it will be quite steam tight, for it is sure to leak a little, as will all the joints, but it may be made so tight as to answer well in practice. In this lid there must be made two 1in. holes, as shown in the figure; one of which, that nearest the rim, must be fitted with a conical wooden plug; and the other, that in the centre, with a short wooden tube made of four pieces of 1in. pine screwed together. This tube is 1in. square inside and 3in. outside, and about 9in. or 12in. long, as is found most convenient. It rests in a little socket made by nailing some pieces on the boiler lid, which form a combing for it. This joint, also the seams of the tube, must be packed with red lead. The steam box is made of 1in. pine screwed together, and should be about 9in. or 12in. wide by 12in. or 15in. high, and at least 10ft. long, though longer would be better; 10ft. is not so long as is required for large carvel built boats, but it is a very convenient length for ordinary small boats and canoes. If a greater length is wanted, it is easy to construct another 10ft. length, and so adjust it as to abut against the other with strips of batten, well red-leaded to cover the joint, but this size box will want a much bigger boiler. One end must be closed in, and the other end provided with a door, which will be kept in its position when in use by a wedge, as shown in Fig. 10; when not in use it comes away, so as to leave a clear opening. To keep the door steam-tight, a packing of leather or indiarubber draught excluder, tacked round its edge, answers very well. On the top of the steam box, at the closed end, a half-inch hole must be made, which will be fitted with a plug to take in and out. This is for testing if the box is full of steam or not; its position is shown in Fig. 10. At the opposite or door end of the steam box in the bottom close to the door must be made a 1in. hole, and this must be fitted with a combing on the outside, just large enough to take the end of the tube rising from the boiler-cover. Inside the steam box there must be cut two rather deep and inclined grooves, running from the sides of the box to the hole in the bottom, so as to run all the condensed steam down into the boiler through the hole and tube. One end of the steam box— the door end—it will be understood from this description, must, therefore, rest on the short wooden tube which rises from the boiler lid, inclining downwards towards it. The opposite or closed end of the steam box is provided with legs, or if the steam box is very long, a horse or trestle of sufficient height is made, and it is rested on this. The horse is placed at such a distance from the boiler as to cause a fair share of the weight to be on the boiler tube; this pressure of course keeps the boiler lid in its place. By this means any pressure can be put on the boiler lid, which acts as a sort of large safety valve.

In using this arrangement the boiler is first very nearly filled through the plug hole, and as it falls short it must be replenished in the same way. Either a wood or a coal fire will answer, and it will be found that a fair supply of steam can be maintained. As a rule, the only parts that will be found to leak steam after the wood has once swollen are the boiler lid and steam box door, but if fairly good work and moderate care have been used in their construction these leaks will not amount to much. When steam is up, which is told by drawing the test plug in the steam box, which will then pass steam, the door is removed, and the box filled with the timber to be steamed, the door being then replaced. In the course of two or three hours any wood that is likely to be wanted by the amateur boat builder will be found to be pliable and soft enough to use. As the steam box is inclined downwards towards the boiler, nearly all the condensed steam returns to it; still the boiler requires replenishing now and then, which is to be done through the hole in the boiler lid, as before described. The height of water in the boiler can always be ascertained by inserting a stick through this hole.

When the amateur requires a curved piece of wood, he had best buy a plank so grained as to enable him to saw it out with the grain; greater strength will thereby be obtained.

A good work bench, fitted with strong vice, will be found very useful in the amateur's boat-shop. A good substitute for it is a long thick plank, say 3in. thick, by 9in. or 12in. wide, by 15ft. or 20ft. long. This may be screwed to a pair of trestles or horses. With the assistance of this, long, narrow, and thin battens can be easily planed. In fitting up a canoe or boat with lockers, a bench expedites work very considerably.

With the foregoing descriptions of the different tools and implements the amateur should be in a position to make many of them for himself, and after a trial or two with the steaming apparatus, he should be in a condition to undertake to build a boat for himself. All this apparatus is not necessary, for it is quite as easy to build a light canoe or skiff without as with steaming. The mode of doing this will be described in due time, attention being only drawn to it here, because perhaps the prospect of being obliged to launch forth into the expense necessary for building a kiln, would prevent some from undertaking the building of a boat.

When the amateur proceeds to design a boat the question of what material shall be used immediately presents itself, and it opens a wide field for inquiry and experiment. Boats are built of very many different woods, varying very much according to the fancy of the builder, who has generally a preference for some particular kind of wood. Some constructors prefer to use two or more different woods in building the hull of their boats, for instance, a different variety above to that which is below the water line, and the latter portion is sometimes of more than one kind. Then, again, in the frames and decks still another variety is used. In building boats with two skins, it is very usual for economy to use a soft wood for the inner and a hard wood for the outer skin, this arrangement often making a very considerable difference in the cost of a boat, especially if a large one. A great deal of this varying of the material is unnecessary, especially in small boats, where very much material is not required, unless there is a desire for decoration. Of course in very light canoe or skiff building more consideration is required, as in these the desideratum of strength with lightness requires much care; and it is also very necessary in constructing boats of a large size, wherein from the quantity of material used the price of it makes a very important item in the expense of building. It is beyond question that it is advisable in building a high class boat, especially if intended for a specific purpose, to use certain kinds of wood in different positions, because many woods from their nature are more suitable for a certain class of work and strain than others. These considerations seldom, however, come under an amateur's notice unless indeed he is a very bold experimenter. There can be no doubt however that these points are worth entertaining; most boat builders disregard them, which is a decided mistake.

The woods generally used in boat building are English and American elm, spruce, larch, mahogany; English, American, and African oak; red pine, white pine, yellow pine, pitch pine, teak, and cedar. Of these, spruce, mahogany, oak, white pine and cedar are more generally used for small clincher built boats, such as skiffs and canoes; while larch, red pine, pitch pine, elm, teak, oak, mahogany, and spruce for carvel built boats, whether for rowing, sailing, or steam launch purposes. There is no rule, however, for the selection of wood, it being very often a mere matter of convenience; but it may be taken as a safe guide that hard woods make the strongest boats, and stand knocking and bumping the best. A short notice of each kind of wood that is most in use will assist the amateur builder in his choice.

Elm, either English or Canadian, is used mostly for keels. It is sometimes used for planking, but other woods are generally preferred for this purpose. It is a very strong and durable wood, easily worked, and holds nails well. It has great transverse strength, and though not very elastic, from its toughness stands knocking about very well. It is very little affected by water, so that it is eminently suited for such positions as keels, or any place where it is subject to the action of bilge water. American elm and ash are largely used for the ribs as frames.

Spruce is a very good wood for light skiffs which are liable to be exposed to the weather and general knocking about. It is light, weighing about 32lb. to the cubic foot, very elastic, and strong. It stands water well, and boats which have been built of it have been known to stand three or four years' work without any paint ever having been put on them at all.

Larch is much the same as spruce, except that it is far more durable and elastic. Light skiffs built entirely of this wood are very satisfactory.

Mahogany is a capital wood for boat building, but it is rather expensive. American mahogany is the best for boats, and it is the easiest for an amateur to work in. Mahogany is exceedingly strong and elastic, and it is not very heavy, and there is no wood which holds a nail so well.

MATERIALS.

Oak is used as keel, stem and stern posts, floors, ribs, or knees; or in the planking or fittings, or even as an oar. However, it is very heavy, weighing from 48lb. to 62lb. a cubic foot. It is very stiff, giving less than any other kind of wood, which is a great advantage in certain kinds of work.

Red pine is an excellent wood. However it is heavy, but then it is very durable, and unrivalled in elasticity. It stands well, and though after some use the fibres which compose its texture rub up a great deal, its toughness makes it very hard to wear. It is easy to work, and is perhaps the best wood an amateur can use for a carvel built boat. It makes very good oars and paddles.

White pine is a very good wood for the planking of light skiffs and canoes. As it only weighs 27lb. to the cubic foot, it is much lighter even than cedar. Its greatest fault is its brittleness, it being the least elastic of any wood used in boat building. It is very easy to work, and of moderate worth.

Pitch pine is a capital wood for boats, partaking of many of the good qualities of larch and spruce, to which it is very closely allied. However, it is rather difficult to work, from its gummy nature.

Teak is of all woods the most suitable for planking carvel built boats of considerable size, as it stands the sun without warping or shrinking; but it is difficult to work, and it is expensive. No wood is more durable, and its strength and elasticity are unsurpassed. It is in itself heavy, but as it is so exceedingly strong, smaller dimensions in the material used are required, so that in using it a light boat is produced. It bends easily, and holds the nails well, while it is practically unaffected by exposure to sun and water.

Cedar is only suited to very small skiffs and canoes, but it is not much used in either, except for decking and similar purposes. Canoes planked with cedar are very light, but as it is addicted to splitting with the grain, and is soft, it is not very good for this purpose. It is not very strong, but as it is tough it stands blows from the striking of a rock or stone fairly well. It is not so much used now for canoes as it was.

White or American cedar, arbor vitæ, a splendid wood for boats and canoes, and for a very light craft it is not to be surpassed, especially for canoes. It is exceedingly light, very tough and pliant, and its durability is everlasting. It is easily worked, and bends easily, but is difficult to get, and expensive.

In choosing the wood for his intended boat, the amateur must be guided very much by his own ideas on the subject, and the opportunity he has for getting suitable wood.

In the selection of the nails there is not so much room for variation, but his judgment will be called in to decide on the stoutness and length of them. There are several kinds of nails, and they are made in copper and iron, these latter being usually galvanised. Copper nails are in every way the best, and, though they cost more, should always be used in skiffs and canoes, but it does not matter so much in punts. Some builders, for economy, in building large boats, use copper nails below the water line and for a few inches above, and then fasten all the rest with iron nails; and under these circumstances they answer very well, especially if the boat is kept well painted. The pattern of nail most in use is the ordinary square boat nail, and the roove, and the clout nail. The ordinary wire nail, or "Point de Paris," will also build a very creditable boat. The boat nail and roove (*a*, Fig. 11) make the strongest and best work, drawing the planking close together, but they are more difficult to use, and entail more work, as each nail, after being driven through, has to have the roove put on, which is done by first cutting the nail to the right length, and then riveting it over the roove. The clout nail (*b*, Fig. 11), which is more like a large tack, is more easy and

MATERIALS.

quicker to use; it is merely driven through the wood, and then the end which projects over is bent into the wood with a tap from the hammer. This nail is almost exclusively used in America, even when so large as four inches in length. In using clout nails, the best plan is to use a nail which is rather long, and, after having bored a hole for it with a very fine bradawl, to gently drive it through the planking up to the head. All but a quarter of an inch of the projecting end should then be cut off with a pair of cutting pincers; and this projecting piece then clouted over and buried into the wood, in the direction of the grain, with the hammer. This makes a very secure and neat job. Fig. 11 gives a representation of each kind of nail when fixed in the boat, the dotted lines showing the portions which are cut off; the amateur can judge from this for himself the security of each kind of nail. Ordinary boat nails are frequently used without the rooves in heavy work, such as the plank and frames of carvel built boats. In selecting nails for a boat, regard must be paid to the thickness of the material they are to hold, stout nails being used for thick wood, and *vice versâ*, otherwise the wood might be split. For all ordinary skiffs Nos. 17 and 15 nails will be found best, with Nos. 1 and 2 burrs or rooves, but much stouter nails than these are required in large boats for sailing or large steam launches. The most useful sizes in length will be found in three-quarter to one and a half inch, varying by quarter inches; these run in price from 2s. 6d. for the smaller to 2s. 2d.

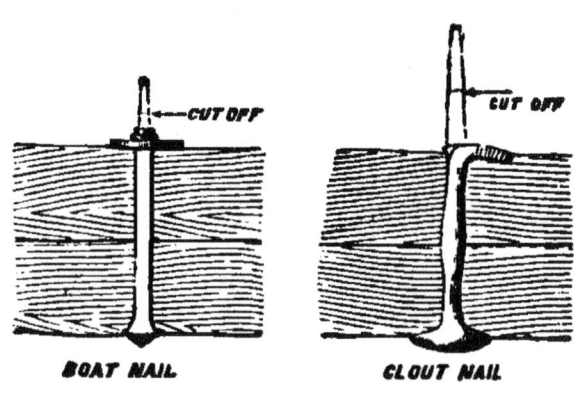

Fig. 11. Boat Nails.

for the larger sizes per pound in copper. Rooves or burrs cost 3s. to 2s. 4d. the pound. Amateurs will find a difficulty in getting boat nails in small quantities, but they can usually be so obtained from Deane and Co., 46, King William-street, London Bridge.

Paints and varnishes for boat work should contain as little turpentine as possible, and in the paints boiled oil should alone be used, otherwise they will not be found to stand water well. For varnish, copal boat varnish should, if possible, always be used, though it is rather expensive, costing 16s. to 18s. per gallon. If this cannot be obtained there is a cheaper kind also called copal boat varnish, but it is a spurious one; the price of this is 12s. a gallon. Either of these will be found to answer very well, but, if they cannot be got, an oil varnish, containing as little turpentine as possible must be used; no spirit varnish will answer at all. Amber varnish will answer, but it is expensive, and requires a long time to dry, but the cheapest and perhaps best that an amateur can do under the circumstance of the absence of varnish, is to paint his boat, and then, when quite dry, to give it a thin even coat of boiled linseed oil. Three good coats of paint outside and two inside a boat make a capital job, and in varnish, two coats inside and out do very well. Some builders use more paint and varnish than this, but it will not be required except for improving the appearance of the work.

CHAPTER III.

PUNTS.

PUNTS are easy to build, requiring no more skill than that possessed by any rough carpenter, for all that is necessary in their construction is strength and water-tight joints. Unlike a skiff, there are no straight planks to be fitted to curved surfaces—always a trying job to the amateur not practised in the proper mode of doing so. In building a punt it is not even necessary that an amateur should possess either tools or accessories beyond a hammer, bradawl, handsaw, and some nails; but the addition of a jack and smoothing plane, tenon saw, rule, square, and bevel will insure quicker and better work. In the material used almost any wood may be selected, and for nails common iron cut nails, if heated to a dull red heat in the fire, and then allowed to cool gradually, will answer very well. These, though answering, are not to be recommended when better can be had; but it is well to draw attention to what will do in case necessity requires their use and no better can be obtained.

In proceeding to design a punt, the first thing to decide on is the purpose it is intended for, which, in this case, I will suppose to be for fishing on a quiet river or lake. For shooting purposes in very shallow flats and marshes, a much lighter punt than the following may be designed. A punt for the purposes mentioned can be heavy, for it is not required to carry it about, comfort, durability, and strength being the first considerations. Having decided on this, the amateur must proceed to fix his

36 *PRACTICAL BOAT BUILDING.*

dimensions, and in this he will find a small sketch greatly help him, as a better impression of their harmony can be so obtained.

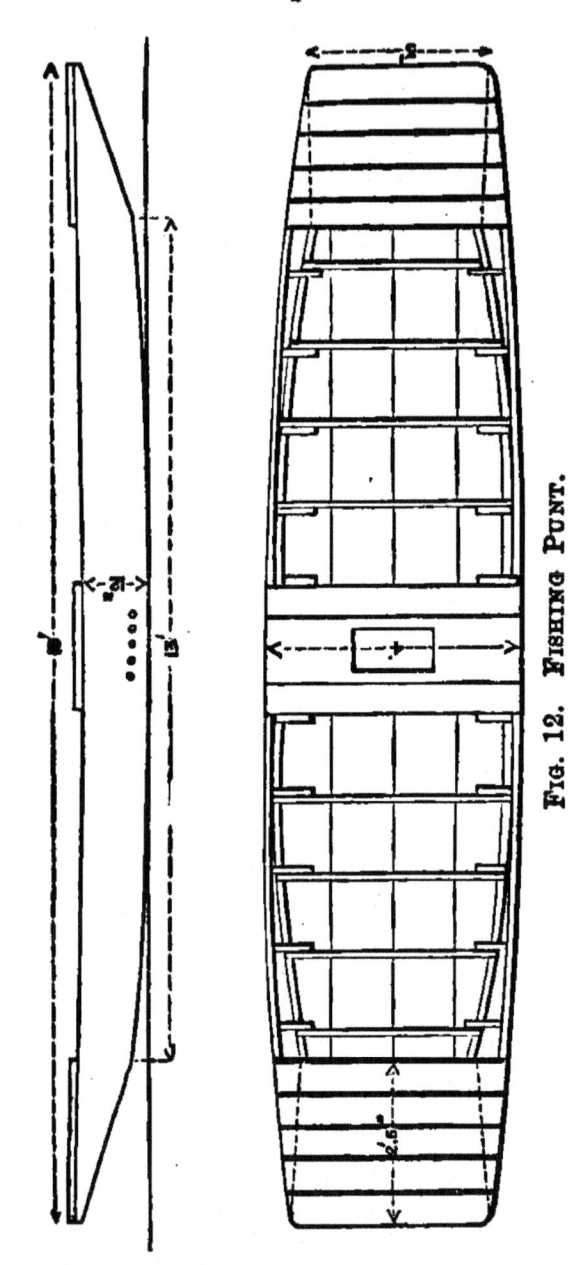

Let the punt be 18ft. long, and this dimension he must mark off on the water-line of his drawing. If he then proceeds to draw a plan he will be better able to form some idea of the width for his punt; let him make this 4ft. outside all. This is making the length four and half times the beam, which is a very good proportion for a fishing punt. For the depth he will find 12in. inside ample, which will make it 13in. deep outside over all. Fig. 12 will give him the proportions of a good fishing punt; this is drawn to a scale of one quarter inch to the foot. The amateur should draw out on a sheet of paper a sketch of the plan and sheer plan like these, but on a larger scale, say, one inch to the foot at least; three inches to the foot would be better.

Fig. 12. Fishing Punt.

PUNTS.

Having fixed on all his dimensions, the material must be selected, and for this red pine or spruce will be found best and cheapest, while for nails, either copper boat nails or galvanised iron hammered nails: though a little more expensive copper nails will be found best. A few strong iron screws will also be wanted. The quantity of wood required will be—two planks 18ft. long, by 1ft. wide by 1in. thick, of good sound red pine, free from knots or shakes; four planks 14ft. long by 1ft. wide by 1in. thick, in spruce or red pine; four ditto 16ft. long by 6in. wide by ¾in. thick, for decking—these last may be of any wood, but spruce or pine had better be obtained. It will save the amateur a great deal of time and trouble, and also the purchasing of tools, if he gets all of them planed for him, and the five 14ft. planks tongued and grooved, and also two of the 16ft. ditto, and all the ¾in. planks. Besides this he will also want some 1in. curly grained elm or oak, or black birch if neither of the others can be got. About twelve feet of this will be enough. His nails must be 2½in. long for all but the decking, 1½in. being required for this. For the decking common cut nails or wire nails will answer very well. For screws he must obtain eight 2½in. iron screws.

Supposing all this material obtained, the amateur must either provide himself with a room or floored shed big enough to hold his boat, or otherwise with two horses or trestles, as shown in Fig. 8, which he had better fasten firmly to the ground, which can easily be done by burying the legs a few inches in the soil. The two 18ft. planks must now be taken and laid one on the top of the other on these horses, and the dimensions for their shape marked out. With his 2ft. rule and pencil let him draw a line from the bottom edge of the plank, 2ft. 6in. from its end, to within one inch of the upper edge and end of the plank, as in Fig. 13. Let him do this at each end on each plank, and neatly

38   *PRACTICAL BOAT BUILDING.*

and squarely saw the triangular piece off. He must now put these two planks aside, and saw off from one of the plain-edged 16ft. planks two pieces 3ft. 10in. long, and make these into a temporary box, the two ends and bottom of which will be here-

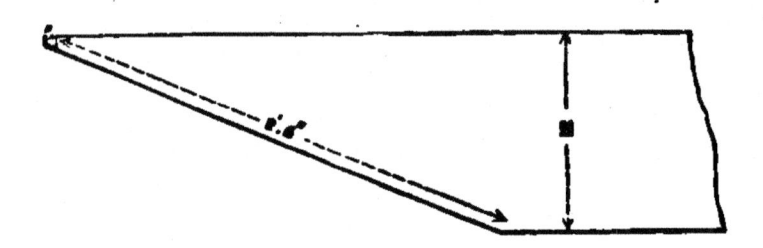

FIG. 13. PLAN OF SIDE PLANK.

after closed in by the sides and bottom of the punt, and the top by the well-decking. These two pieces must therefore be temporarily fastened together with any odd strips of wood. They

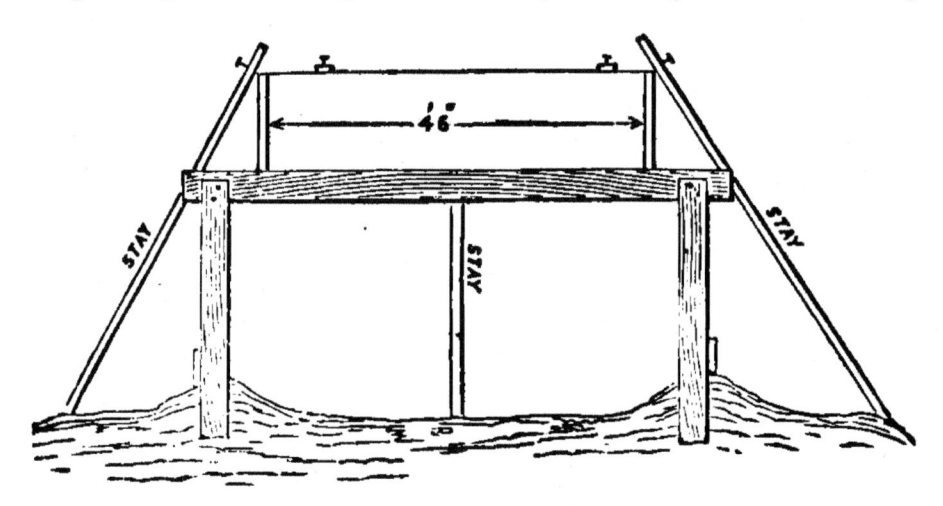

FIG. 14. PUNT BUILDING.

must be spaced 2ft. apart, and must be exactly square with each other. Now take up the side planks and fix them with a light stay and tack, as shown in Fig. 14, on to the trestles, exactly 3ft. 10in. apart, and *upside down*. Great care must be taken

PUNTS. 39

that they are exactly true to each other, that both are on the same level and are perpendicular, and that they tally with each other in length.

Now take the box and place it exactly into the centre of the length of the planks, across the punt, where it should fit nicely. This must be temporarily supported in its place, which may be done by a stay from below it (see Fig. 14). Now screw in a 2½in. screw through the side plank into each side piece of the box, about 2in. from the top edge, and another again about 3in. from the bottom edge. The box will thus be fixed in its position, where it will be now a permanent midship frame to the punt.

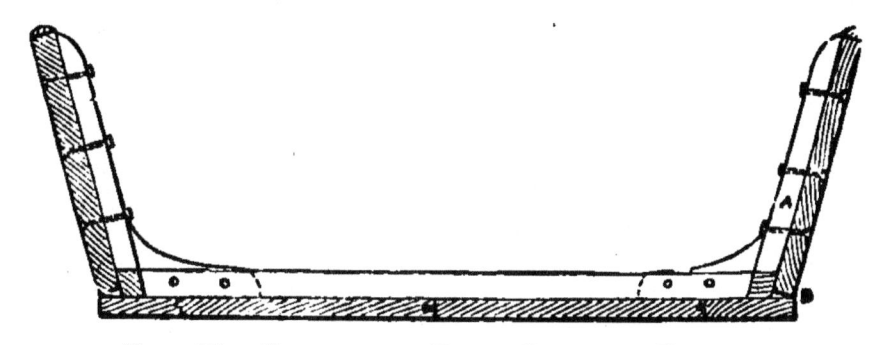

FIG. 15. SECTION OF PUNT SHOWING FRAMES.

Take any two odd pieces of wood and nail them lightly on to the top side of the side planks, keeping them just 3ft. asunder over all, and with two more pieces draw in the bottom edge of the planks, fastening each piece of wood so as to keep them about 2ft. 6in. apart. This drawing of the planks together will give a good shape to the punt.

The frames, which are really the foundation and strength of the punt, must now be put in. To do this, saw out a lot of 1in. stuff 1in. square for bottom strips; about 84ft. run will be wanted for this, and it should be planed up on all sides. The amateur must now cut out of his hard wood plank twenty knees, like A in Fig. 15; the angle of each pair of these will vary, but, with the help of his bevel-square, he will easily ascertain this by measuring the angle of the side planks and a board laid across at each position of the frames. These frames are placed 15in. apart from centre to centre, the first starting from the side of the well. This allows of four frames on each side of the well. These angles should be alike for similar positions at each end of the punt, but it is seldom that such accuracy is used in construction as to make them so. If the amateur can do it, that is, get the material, he can put in light iron knees instead of these wooden ones; but the wooden ones, if carefully selected, so that the grain runs as far as possible with the curve, and for some little distance up the long arm of the knee, will make the best work.

Going now to the framework of the punt on the trestles, he must first proceed to put in the side stringers, which run the whole length of the bottom of the punt, on each side, to strengthen it. These are made of the 1in. pine that has been sawn out. He must select two pieces of this that will bend easily, and which are about 13ft. 6in. long. Each of these he must carefully nail inside the punt, along the bottom edge of the side planks, so that they may project a little beyond $\frac{1}{8}$th of an inch. This is done so that when the bottom of the punt is put on there may be a little recess between itself and the side plank and stringer for the caulking, as is shown at B, Fig. 15. In nailing these on, the nails must be placed about 6in. apart, being driven in from the outside, and the rooves put on and riveted before proceeding any further. The two planks forming the well will interfere with the placing of these two stringers, so they must each have a small recess cut into them, to allow the stringers being placed. The bottom frames and side frames must now be put in, and in doing this the amateur must exercise some care, or otherwise they may not all be on the same level, which would bother him when putting on the bottom. Let him first mark out their position, commencing first at the well, and placing each at 15in. from the other. This will allow him to put in four on each side of the well, or five on each side of the centre of the boat, including the one at the well. Let him put in each pair complete, that is, the two side frames and the bottom frame, before he proceeds to put in another pair. With the assistance of a light batten slightly tacked to the well and used as a gauge, he can easily keep them all in their proper level. This batten should be nailed so as to go along the centre line of the boat, and must be used in the following manner: First, nail on with two nails each to the side plank, each side frame by the well; these nails must not be rooved or clinched as yet. Also drive two nails through into the short arm, and two nails into the long arm of each knee from inside the well, and roove and rivet these. Be sure that the bottom of the frames are on a level with the stringers, that is, projecting about $\frac{1}{8}$th of an inch beyond the well boards. Do this for each side of the well. Now cut off two pieces of the 1in. strip of pine, of just sufficient length to fit nicely between the stringers when lying against the inside of the well boards, but projecting beyond them on the same level as the stringers and knees. Nail these firmly on to the well, the nails 6in. apart. The batten before mentioned to be used as a gauge must now be laid on and nailed lightly to these two bottom frames in their centre. He must now proceed to treat each set of frames in the same way, not clinching any of the nails till he has made sure that all the frames are right, which, if he finds it to be the case, he must then go over again, rooving and riveting all the nails firmly. The bottom frames should all be put on the same sides of the side frames, so that the spaces between them may be even; and if as each bottom frame is put on the gauge batten is lightly tacked to it, the amateur will be sure to have all right.

42 PRACTICAL BOAT BUILDING.

The amateur must now proceed to finish the ends, and, as these are straight, the gauging batten will be of no use to him, but he will find a straight edge of service as a guide. First of

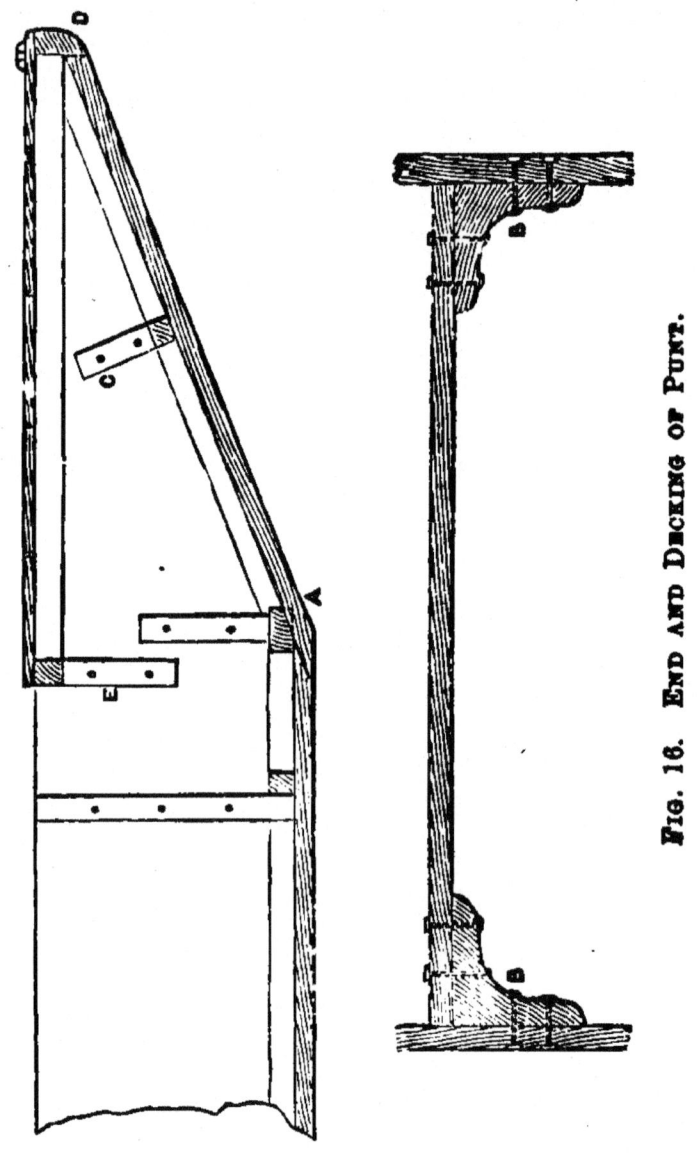

FIG. 16. END AND DECKING OF PUNT.

all he must prepare four pieces of wood, 1in. thick by 2in. wide, and about 2ft. 6in. long. These must be planed on all sides. He must also make twelve hard wood knees, 1in. thick and 6in. long on each side, of the shape shown in B, Fig. 16. Let him now

PUNTS.

take one of the two 1in. pieces, and saw it off such a length that it shall fit firmly between the stringers at A, Fig. 16. This must be placed so as to project a little beyond the bevel of the side planks, as shown by the dotted lines at A, and on a level with the stringers. To secure this in its place, nail a hard wood knee on each end of it, as shown in B, Fig. 16, with two nails, and nail the knee to the side planks. Now put in a 1in. strip of pine on each side, plank up the bevel to act as the stringers along its bottom, and then fasten it to frame C of 1in. strip and D of 1in. by 2in. strip. This latter projects beyond the side planks, as marked off by the dotted lines at D. Frame C is half-way between the frames A and D. With the help of the straight-edge these must be made level. The nails of these must be all rooved and riveted. Each end must be thus treated. This being all finished, it is time to put in the bottom. Take the 14ft. planks, and, after seeing that they are all good and sound, and not curled up, take one of them, and, laying it carefully down the centre of the punt, so that one of its edges coincides with the centre line of the punt, nail it lightly on to the well board frames with one nail in each to the centre of the board. Bore the holes for these nails, and for all that go through the bottom planks, with a rather fine bradawl, otherwise the plank may be split, which will, as a matter of course, give much trouble. Now bring the plank down on to the frames at each end of the punt, and secure it there with a nail lightly driven in as before. If this lies on the frames all right, take another and lay it on in a similar way; but on the other half of the punt, being careful to fit the tongueing and grooving very closely, and, above all things, not to split off the edges of the planks. Recollect that all these planks are tongued and grooved.

Now put on the two side planks with the same care; but exercise a little judgment in placing the nails at the ends, where the planks narrow on account of the taper of the bottom of the punt. The ends of all the planking will project over a little at each end of the punt; but this is no matter, all the amateur has to do now is to see that the bottom lies closely and evenly on to the bottom frames, and that the tongues and grooves go home and fit close. If the amateur has it, he may give the tongues and grooves a coat of rather thick paint just before he puts them together; but he must be careful not to put in too much, or they will not close together. If all the bottom fits right, he must go over it, and put in two more nails through each plank where it crosses a frame. Let him put the nails as close to the edge of the plank as he can safely do without splitting it—about 1¼in. to 1½in.; but where the side planks are very narrow at the ends, as before remarked, judgment must be used, as perhaps only two nails can be well put in.

The punt must now be turned on its side or bottom, as found most convenient, and the assistance of someone obtained while the amateur proceeds to roove and rivet all these nails. His assistant will be required to back up the nails with a very heavy hammer, or, what is better, a light anvil of the shape shown in A, Fig. 17. In hammering the nails in, or riveting them, a very light hammer is wanted. To drive the rooves on to the nails close down to the wood a tool will be required like a punch with a hole or pipe in it.

This being done, turn the punt back again, and proceed to saw off the ends of the planks and the end frame, as shown at A, Fig. 16; and also saw off the frame D, as shown in the same figure. Now put in the ends, as the bottom was put in, and rivet up the ends of the nails as before.

The chief work of the punt is now complete, all that now remains to be done being the caulking, painting, and fitting.

The first step is the caulking of the seams in the bottom, and

PUNTS. 45

for doing this the amateur will require a caulking iron and mallet, but he can do it very well with a wood caulking chisel, made of hard wood, and any light mallet with a springy helve. If he makes them as shown in B and C, Fig. 17 they will answer very well. The dimensions of the chisel are given, and for material a piece of his oak plank will do. In preparing his pitch he must melt it over a gentle fire, with a little tallow, several pounds of pitch in a pot, and he must keep it well stirred, and be careful that it does not catch fire. When it is well melted

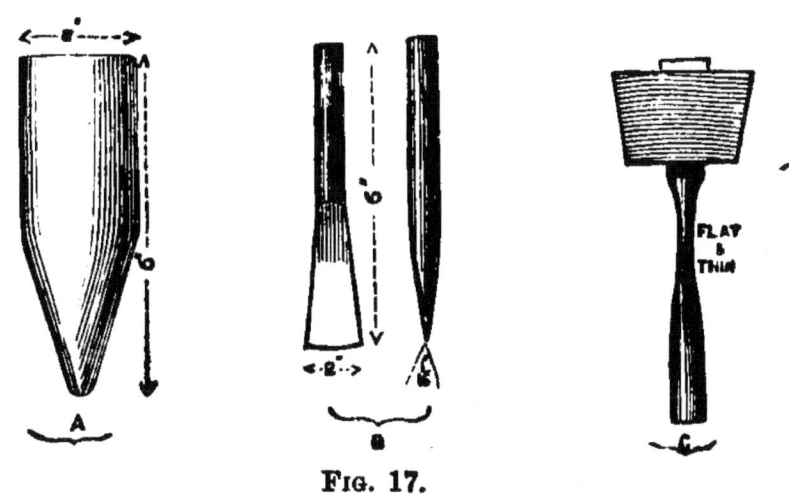

FIG. 17.

A. LIGHT ANVIL.   B. CAULKING CHISEL.   C. CAULKING MALLET.

he must test its quality by dipping a little stick in it, and cooling the pitch that adheres to it in cold water. If the little drop that hangs from the stick breaks brittly it shows that there is not sufficient tallow in it, so more must be added and well mixed in; if the drop is soft and sticky pitch must be added, for there is too much tallow—and so on till he gets it to the right temper. One or two trials will render the amateur an expert. If he cannot get pitch he may use resin; but to the resin he must add, as well as the tallow, about an equal quantity of lampblack or powdered wood charcoal; but pitch prepared in this way requires far more skill in its manipulation. Having spun his oakum into a loose cord of a size that will fit nicely into the seam or crevice to be stopped when it is compressed under the mallet (his judgment must be exercised to determine this), he must dip it piece by piece into the hot pitch and saturate it, and then drive it into the openings hard and firm with sharp, quick, and elastic blows of his chisel and mallet. It takes a good deal of experience to caulk well and neatly, and the operation necessary is very difficult to describe; but a few trials will soon put the amateur in the way of doing it. He must fill the cracks quite full, going over them two or three times if necessary; but this must always be avoided as much as possible, because each time risks breaking that which was first put in. If a hole is very large, requiring a good deal of caulking, it may be done by first almost filling it with dry oakum, and then driving in the pitched oakum. The chisel will be constantly sticking to the oakum and drawing it out of the seams between the blows of the mallet. This must be obviated by having a small vessel of oil at hand into which the point of the chisel will be dipped when it shows a tendency to stick.

The seams that have to be pitched are the seams on each side of the punt, along the bottom edge of the side planks, also the seams formed by the well-boards and the frames, and any cracks that may show themselves in the bottom and end planking. Afterwards he may give inside the boat a thin coat of pitch, with a brush, all over the inside of the well, and along the joints of the side stringers, with the sides and bottom, and also the joints of the end frame with the bottom and end planking. When this is all hard and dry he must dress off all surplus pitch with a sharp chisel well oiled, and then give the inside of the punt a good coat of paint, filling up all the little cracks and joints.

The amateur must now make the decks for the ends and well. In decking in the ends the amateur must first of all put in a piece of wood, 1in. by 2in. deep, 2ft. 6in. from each end of the punt, and across it from side to side. This must have a knee of hard wood at each end, and by them secured to the side planks. (See E, Fig. 16.) From the centre of this another piece 1in. square must be mortised, the other end being mortised to the frame D at the nose of the punt. This must be done for each end of the punt. The three-quarter inch planking must now be taken and cut into proper lengths and nailed on to the side planks and the frame, the ½in. nails being used. This decking will be laid across the punt from side to side, and, as it is all tongued and grooved, it must be made to fit well before the nails are finally driven home. Each piece of planking for the decks may receive a coat of paint on its lower surface before being nailed in its place. In decking the well exactly the same process must be used, 1in. cross pieces being put in from one well board to the other to form a support for the well-hole cover. The well-hole should be 1ft. 3in. long by 9in. wide.

If the amateur wishes to put in any fittings, he must now do it, and should he intend to iron the nose it must now be done. This is not necessary, unless the punt is intended for knocking about much. A piece of oak ½in. thick and 1in. deep, secured as a stringer all along the top of the side planks and round the ends, will be a great improvement, as it saves the planking from roughing up when poling. Having thoroughly inspected his work—observing that all the nails are properly clinched, and that there are no rough, untidy corners—the amateur may decide to paint it and finish up.

For painting, dark grey or green is the best colour. For painting a punt of this size, giving it three good coats outside and two inside, about one gallon, or 12lb. to 14lb. of prepared paint will be wanted. With a good-sized brush let him give all the inside that he can get at a good coat of paint, rubbing it well in.

The punt may then be turned over and the outside receive a coat. When this is thoroughly dry a second coat may be given, which should be allowed to dry well and hard for, say, at least five days. The outside may then receive a third coat, put on very thin, and this coat must be allowed to dry thoroughly, say from seven to ten days. When painting, if any rough places show themselves, they may be rubbed down with sand-paper.

This completes the punt, and if the amateur is but a moderate carpenter, and has exercised a fair amount of care, he will have succeeded in making a craft that will be very serviceable and durable for many years, yet not so heavy or clumsy as those usually found at the river side.

CHAPTER IV.

CLENCH-BUILT SKIFFS.

HAVING shown how a punt is to be built, in this chapter a description of and how to build a skiff will be given. It is impossible to enter into an account of more than one kind of skiff in a handbook so brief as this, as there are very many different varieties made, and they are known under as many different names. For instance, a wherry, a galley, an outrigger, a dingy, or even a pinnace, are all so many different kinds of skiffs, for under this heading comes any small boat which is light, and is propelled by one or more oarsmen, not more than one sitting on each seat.

The same *modus operandi* that is required in building a punt is also brought into play in building a skiff, that is, designs must be first got out, then material selected, and then the general routine of building. In a skiff, however, infinitely more skill is required, some knowledge beyond mere carpentry being brought into action. In a punt nearly all, in fact, practically all, the work is angular. In a skiff this is different, for, with a few exceptions, there is not a square or angular joint in it, all the joints being the junction of one circular surface to another. It is in this peculiarity that the difficulty of boat building proper lies.

The first step in building a skiff or any boat is for it to be decided how and for what it is to be used. More depends on this than would at first sight appear; for instance, a little consideration will show that if a skiff is to be used on a lake or an estuary, it must be designed for rather rougher water than if it was only required on a quiet river. Also in an estuary tides flowing in and out will often make the labour of pulling a boat rather severe work; therefore, if it be possible to put on a small sail now and again, so much the better. A skiff intended only for river work need not be either as strong or as steady, nor need it be so seaworthy; so that a longer, narrower, and outrigged boat will answer every purpose. If it is to be used for shooting or fishing, or camping out, alterations in design again creep in, according to the purpose for which it is intended. As a long thin boat is easier to design and build than a short bluff one, and also as a sailing boat will be hereafter described, we will take the former class as a model for our design, selecting that material which will make a thoroughly good, if not a very cheap, boat.

The lines for a river skiff of this class should be sharp and clean, to produce which the boat must not be too broad in proportion to its length. Let the amateur get his drawing board and paper, and as his design must be fairly clean, a good scale must be chosen—say, not less than one inch to the foot. On this scale for the following designs a sheet of imperial cartridge will do very well. The general dimensions must then be fixed upon, which in this case will be

Length over all	28ft.
,, on water line	28ft.
Beam over all	4ft.
,, on water line	3ft. 4in.
Distance of midship frame from bow	16ft.
Depth at bow	20in.
,, midship frame	16in.
,, stern	18in.

In this the length is to the beam as 7 to 1. This is not so fine as a light outrigger, but quite fine enough for a good general rowing boat. Besides, if longer than this, the amateur would find some difficulty in getting wood that would run the whole length of his craft without jointing. Let the designer refer back to the chapter which refers to designing boat lines, and get a selection of the instruments he will require. There is no absolute need to design his skiff first, but it will in all probability save a world of trouble afterwards. The first and most important essential in the design of a skiff is that it should have a moderately flat floor, with a rapidly increasing displacement, so that in the first place it should draw but little water, and in the second place that it should roll or cant to one side evenly and steadily when its occupants should move about. In Fig. 18 are the designs for a midship frame and bow and stern frames for a skiff of this size. The amateur must use all his skill in designing these, for, if they are faulty and not true to each other, he cannot hope to make his skiff without a great deal of trouble.

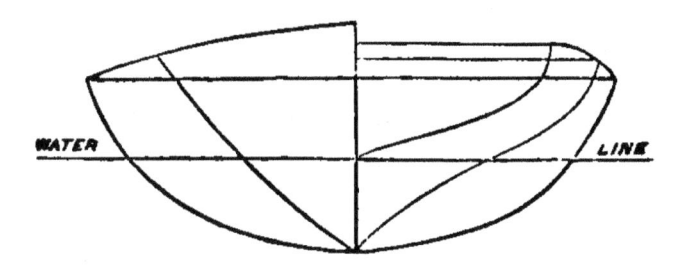

FIG. 18. DESIGNS FOR MIDSHIP, BOW, AND STERN FRAMES FOR SKIFF.

Having drawn out his plans completely, he must proceed to make his moulds to build on. Each of these must be made on the principle shown in Fig. 9, Chapter II. If made of one inch pine, and finally braced together, they will answer very well.

First, the keel has to be got out. Take a piece of elm, English or American, of the required length (27ft. 6in.), and 2½in. by 4in. The next step will be to cut the rabbet for the garboard plank. The rabbet will be cut ½in. from the upper side of the keel, and be deep enough to take the edge of the garboard and a good nail fastening. If the bottom of the boat be nearly or quite flat, the keel can be constructed as shown in Fig. 19 or 20, A being the plank.

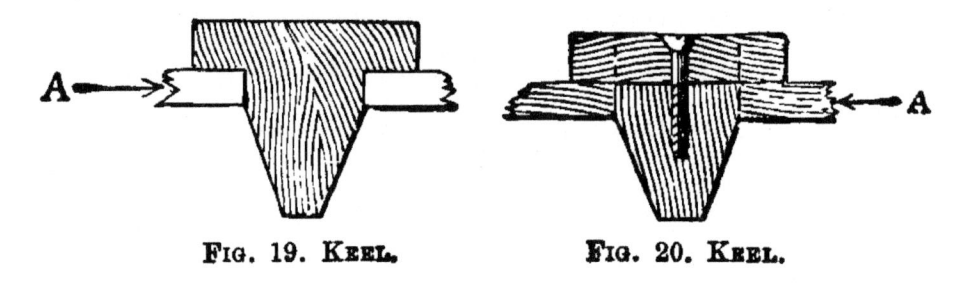

FIG. 19. KEEL. FIG. 20. KEEL.

The rabbet along the keel having been cut out with a chisel, the builder will proceed to fit the stem and stern post.

For the stem a good sound clear grained piece of oak must be selected, which, if possible, should have such graining as to allow of the forefoot to be cut out with it, as is shown in A, Fig. 21. In B in this same figure the forepart is not so cut out, but in that way of fitting the stem on to the keel it does not matter so much. In Fig. 21, A and B are two different ways of fitting the stem to the keel, A being suited to large boats with keels from 3in. to 4in. wide on the face, but it answers very well in small boats, especially if it is used with a flat band all round the curve and along the keel. It is simply a box scarf joint divided down the middle of the keel with two small wood pins to keep it in place, and a hard wood knee in the angle to stiffen the joint. In B the joint is a tenon recessed into the stem piece, stiffened like A with wood knee, which is always broader at the back than in front (see D) to help support the plank. Either answers very well, and in very small boats are often dispensed with, the keel simply biting against the stem and the two secured together by a brace or angle iron. The amateur will see that the plan shown in A is the easiest to make, and it answers

CLENCH-BUILT SKIFFS.

every purpose. C in Fig. 21 shows the front view of the stem, and D a sectional plan cut through near the top on the line *a-b*. In this view *a* and *b* are the ends of the planking nailed to the stem. The stem piece must of course be rabbeted.

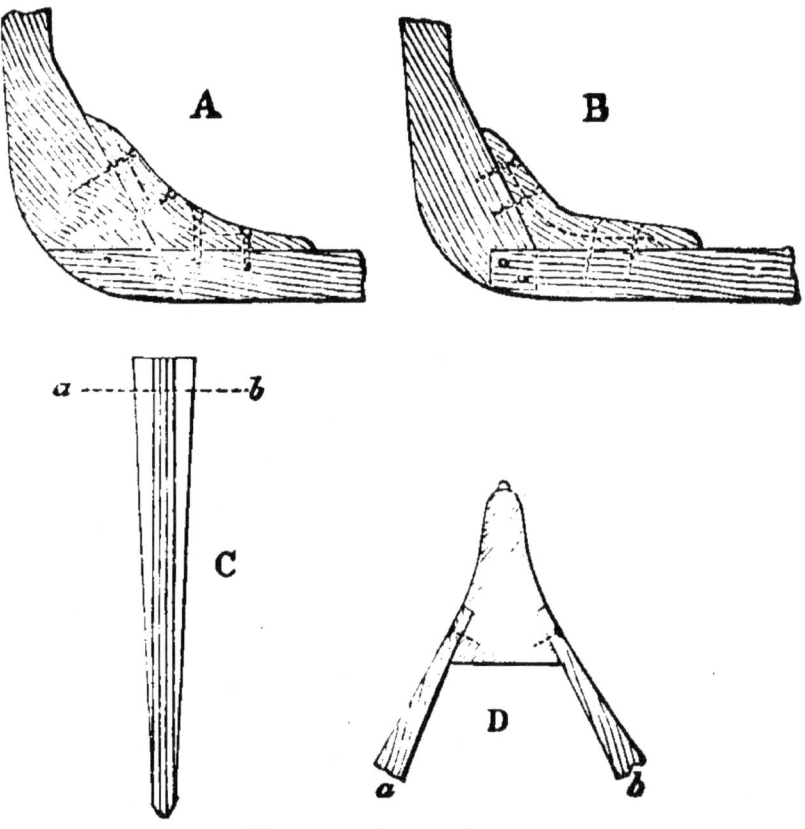

FIG. 21. STEM PIECES.

Fig. 22 shows the stern post, which may be mortised in, as shown by this figure, and secured with two pins and an angle iron (A) as shown, or a wood knee; or the stern post can be box scarfed. These having been securely fixed in their positions on the keel, the whole frame of stem, keel, and stern post must be taken and fitted to the building stock or trestle. The stem and stern post must be plumbed upright and secured by stays of wood to the ceiling or floor of the workshop, also a stringer of wood should be nailed from stem head to head of stern post. The keel must next be secured to the building stock. Nail cleats of wood on each side of the deal about 2ft. 6in. apart, and reaching above the deal to within ¾in. of the lower edge of the rabbet. As the keel will not be so wide as the deal stocks, wedges can be used to jam the keel tight in the cleats on the keel. In the first place stretch a stout line from inside stem to inside stern post, to represent the load water line. The keel, &c., must be so fixed on the stocks that the L.W.L. comes perfectly horizontal under a spirit level test. Mark the load water line on each of the moulds; then square the moulds to the stretched line representing the load water line, and plumb

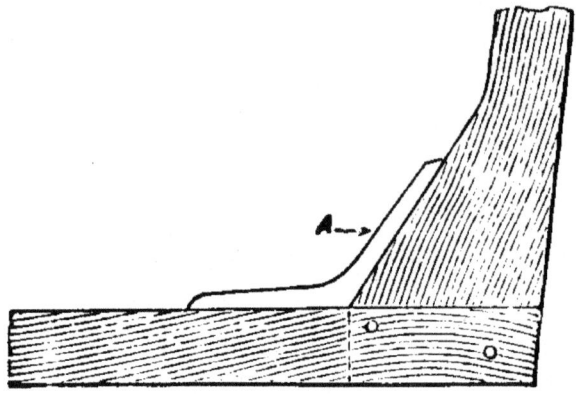

FIG. 22. STERN POST, WITH MORTICE AND KNEE.

The moulds must now be fixed in position

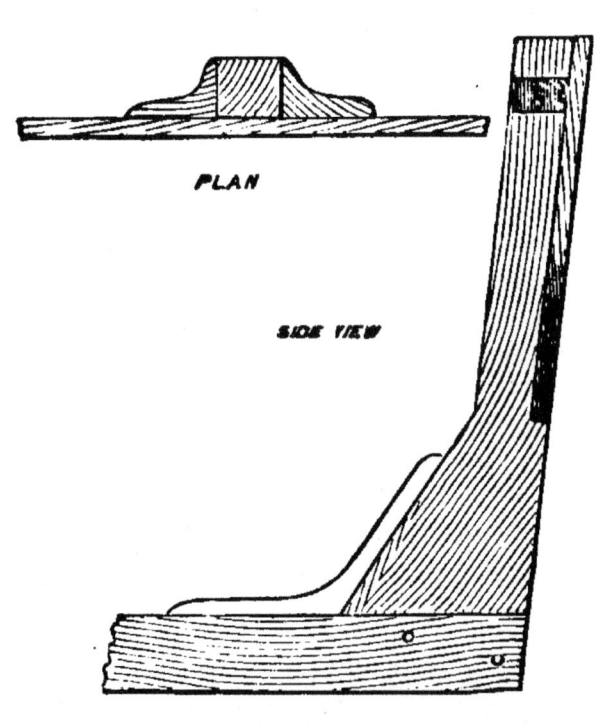

FIG. 23. FIXING THE STERN PIECE.

them upright. The moulds will be kept in position by wood stays (the same as the stem and stern post), and by a temporary gunwale strake. The transom will be fitted to the stern post at the time the moulds are put into place.

Now take some ¾in. material, mahogany or elm, as the case may be, and plane it up. It should be of such a depth that when laid across the stern post there will not be any joint in it. If of necessity there must be a joint, this ought to be tongued and grooved, as in the bottom of the joint as described in Chapter III. Cut away the stern post as shown in Fig. 23, and, with some 2in. screws or stout iron nails, fasten the transom firmly in its place. Three screws will be sufficient, with the addition of two iron or wooden knees on the inside, as shown. Care must be taken to get this stern piece or transom in perfectly true and square. Secure the temporary gunwale strake to the transom, and, if necessary, put a stay to each side of the stern to steady it.

As the frame now stands, it is in the condition that is necessary to receive the planking. Planking is the most difficult portion of the work, and if the amateur can get someone to help to hold the planking, &c., it will be of great assistance to him. Sometimes, if the plank is not long enough, it is impossible to plank a frame with continuous strips from bow to stern. In such a case a long feather edge scarf has to be made. This plan gives far more work. The scarf joints must be made as long as possible, and a piece of Stockholm tarred or white-leaded paper put between them. The scarfs will be secured by small copper nails properly clenched. In all cases the overlap of the scarf should be in the direction of the stern *on the outside*, so that if the feather edge became jagged no weeds, &c., would be picked up. Sometimes a scarf is necessary if a continuous plank of the required curve cannot be met with.

The plank should be ⅜in., or ½in. of cedar, pine, or mahogany. Each plank should be not greater than 5in. in width, but if the turn of the bilge is very sharp, narrower planking should be used in this part, otherwise it will not be got round the bilge.

Mark off on the midship mould spots where the edges of the plank will come, observing, as judgment suggests, that narrower planks may be required at the bilge. Mark an *equal* number of spots on the other moulds, and on the stem and stern post. The distances between these spots will, of course, become more contracted towards the bow and stern. Take a plank of about 5in. in width, and fit it carefully into the rabbet to form the garboard strake. When fitted on its lower edge into the rabbet, secure it at the stem piece and stern post by an overlapping cleat nailed to stem and stern post. [Whilst fitting in the garboard strake it will be found very convenient to have an assistant to "hold on."] When the garboard strake is adjusted in the rabbet mark carefully towards its upper edge where the "spots" on the moulds and on the stem and stern post come. Remove the strake, run a line in through the spots, and saw down the line. The line will be found to be more or less curved. Plane up the strake and nail it into the rabbet.

Take a gauge and set to $\frac{3}{4}$in. Run the gauge along the top edge of the garboard strake on the outside, and the line marked will represent the overlap of the next strake. Take the plank out of which the next strake is to be cut, and fit it round to overlap the top edge of the garboard. Mark on the plank with a pencil run along the top edge of the garboard the shape of the curve. Remove the plank and saw to the curved line. Fit the plank again, but this time to the $\frac{3}{4}$in. overlap marked on the garboard; mark on the plank where the "spots" for the next strake come. Remove the plank, run a line in through the "spots" so marked, and saw down the line. The second strake will now be formed; plane it up, and fit it over the top edge of the garboard with the $\frac{3}{4}$in. overlap. The ends of the strake

CLENCH-BUILT SKIFFS.

should be bevelled away to almost a feather edge at stem and stern post, so that the strakes here at their load ends finish in the rabbet to look almost like carvel build. If this is not done, the work will look very clumsy, and the rabbet in the stem and stern post will have to be very deep. The strake, whilst being nailed, can be kept in position at the stem and stern by cleats, as before described, but for the intermediate part it will be found convenient to use clamps. These clamps are of very simple construction:

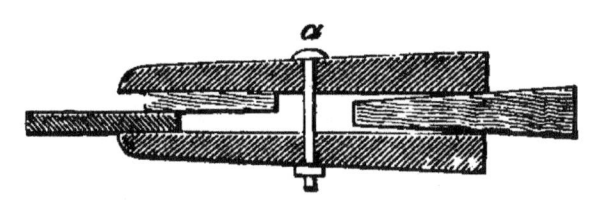

FIG. 24. CLAMP.

Take two pieces of hard wood, about 10in. long and 2½in. square, as shown in Fig. 24. Connect them loosely by a nut bolt, *a*. Place the claw of the clamp over the lands of the strakes and wedge up. Several of these clamps will be required, and each strake can be additionally secured by temporary nails to the moulds. The strakes will be nailed and rooved together along the overlap at intervals of from 2in. to 3in.

When the turn of the bilge is approached, take a smoothing

FIG. 25. FIG. 26. FIG. 27. FIG. 28.
PLANKING.

plane and bevel off the edge, as is shown in Fig. 25. This is done to make the next plank lie snug on the one that preceded it, as is shown in Fig. 26; otherwise it would lie as in Fig. 27. The bevelling must be done till the edge of the plank is reduced to about half its full thickness, if it is required, but never less.

With a little practice the amateur will be able to bevel this off very quickly and neatly, guided by the eye alone; but at first, in all probability, he will require a guide. Of course, most of the bevelling is required at the midship frame, because it is there that most of the curve of the planking lies, little or no bevelling being required on this account at the stem, but more may be required at the transom. However, some builders bevel the planks at the bow in all fine-built boats, but this is done simply for appearance, as it makes a neater finish; but at the bilge both edges of the planks must be bevelled. Fig. 28 shows this arrangement. All the nails must have holes bored for them before being put in. When the amateur comes to the last plank or top strake he may either put on a stouter one, at least one-half thicker, or he may put on a separate piece outside, and along the top edge of the gunwale, in which case he must first clinch all the nails. The amateur must now get an assistant, or holder on, to help him clinch or roove all the nails.

The ribs must now be put in, and, as there are several ways of doing so, illustrations are given in Figs. 29 and 30 to show the different plans. In the plan shown in Fig. 29 all the ribs are sawn out of the plank the right size and shape, $\frac{3}{4}$in. oak, American or elm plank being used. As far as possible the curve of the rib should run with the grain of the wood, but it is not to be expected that it will do so completely. This plan is almost always used in skiffs and fine boats, the long ribs being placed from 15in. to 18in. apart, with a short rib or floor extending about two-thirds of the length of the others, spaced halfway between each. In securing these in their places one nail is driven through each plank, through the rib where it is rooved and riveted, in this boat the same nails being used as in the planking, the dotted line x showing the position of this nail; but sometimes two are used, in which case they serve

CLENCH-BUILT SKIFFS.

to secure the stringers *a b c* as well—the dotted lines *z z* indicate where they are then placed. In the plan shown in Fig. 29 the

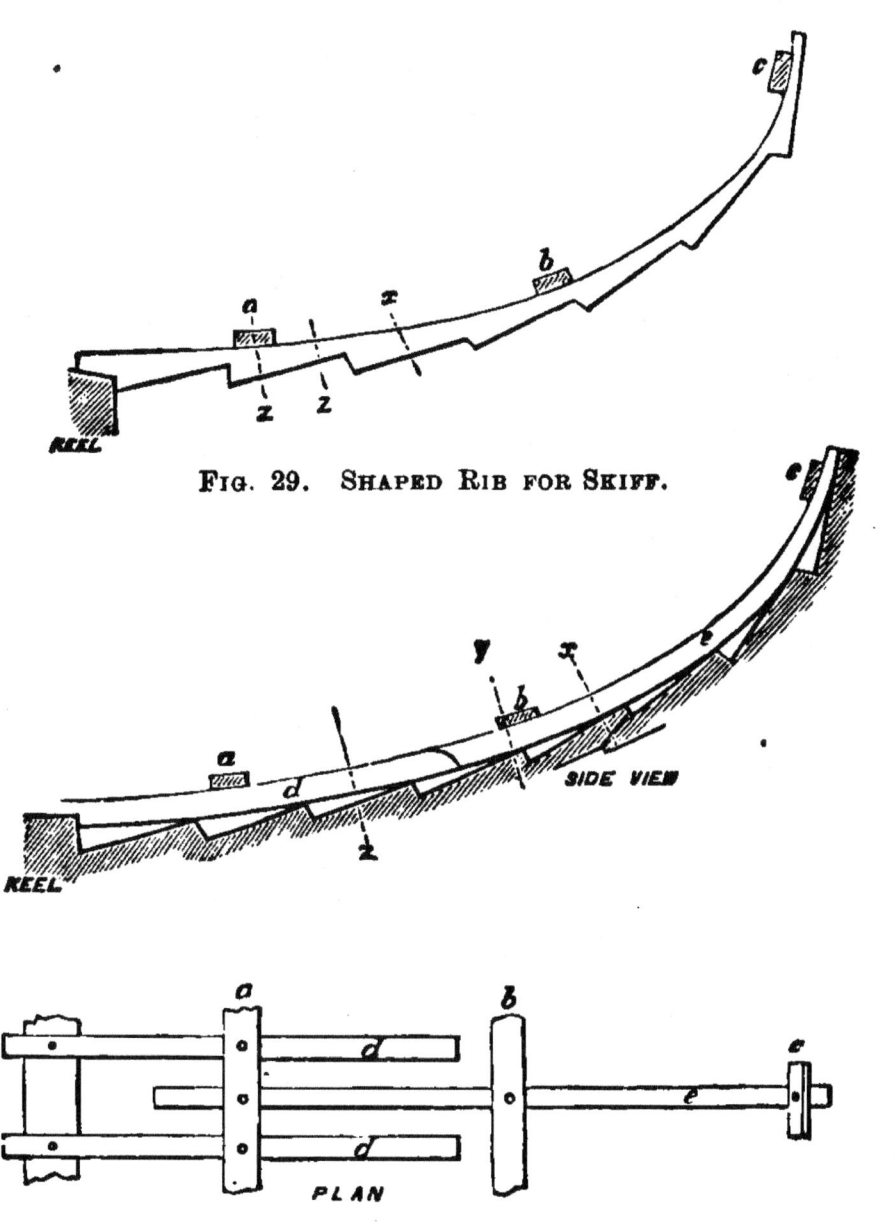

FIG. 29. SHAPED RIB FOR SKIFF.

FIG. 30. RIB AND FLOOR OF SKIFF.

ribs are made of American elm strips sawn out from ⅜in. to ⅝in. thick, and ¾in. or ¼in. wide. In most boats these will go into position without any preparation, but in some it will be necessary to soften them with either steam or boiling water. The nails are best when driven right through both planks into the rib, and then rooved and riveted as in x, but they are more frequently driven in as in z. In spacing these in a boat, about 12in. or 15in. must be allowed between the single frames, and then a floor frame placed about 1in. to 2in. on each side of this. These floor frames run right across the boat, so that they extend on each side of the keel. Often the floors are joggled as shown in the side view to fit in the overlapping or lands of the plank, but it weakens the ribs to joggle them. The longitudinal stringers, *a b c*, are often spaced so as to be bound by the nail that runs through the planking and ribs, as is shown by the dotted line y and the stringer b in the side view. The lower stringer a should always bind the floor frames $d\,d$ and the single frames e together, as is shown in the plan, Fig. 30. At the entrance or bow the frames cannot always be extended across, as they break rather than bend sufficiently; in this case they are cut and run further up the side of the boat. In any boat that is intended to be extra strong it is well to place the ribs much closer at the bows, extending some way back, say the first 6ft. spaced open, and then for the next 4ft. spaced close, as in the example before us.

Bent timbers of oak, ash, or American elm are commonly used as ribs for small boats, and they are seldom joggled, as cutting across the grain is almost certain to cause the bent timber to "fly" between joggle and joggle. The timbers must be got out of clean stuff of the proper size (viz., ¾in. square) and length, to go from gunwale to gunwale. They must be put into the steam kiln, and allowed to remain steaming until they are sufficiently pliant. The stations for the timbers must be marked on keel and gunwale, and across the plank. This is usually done by bending a thin batten inside the boat across the plank at the station for the timber, and then marking along the edge of the latter with chalk or pencil. The holes for the nails will next be bored through the plank on the line for the timbers. Take a batten out of the steam kiln and bend it down to the keel with the foot; secure it to the keel with a stout nail, next bend it to the plank over the holes already bored. Drive the nails through the timbers, and clinch or roove the nails on the face of the timber. No holes need be bored through the timbers if the nails can be got through without. The holes in the plank should be small, so that the nails will make a tight fit, otherwise the boat will soon become "nail sick." An assistant will be necessary whilst the timbers are being put in.

After the bent timbers are in, "floors," extending up to near the turn of the bilge, should be put in. These floors will be 1in. in width, and 1¾in. deep at the "throat,"—*i.e.*, the part on the keel. They should be sawn out of oak (crooked grained, to suit the bend, if possible), and should be joggled, as shown in Fig. 29. They should have a piece cut out, ½in. deep, to fit over the top of the keel; but a small waterway, or hole, should be left between the floor and the garboard.

The stringers and seats must now be put in. The ribs must be cut down to 1¼in. below the top strake. A gunwale of 1¼in. square (American elm) is then fitted round and over the rib heads, and then fastened to the top strake. Sometimes an outside gunwale or rubbing piece is fitted as well. Wherever a seat is to be put in, another rib to support must be placed. Let the first seat be about 4ft. from the bows, and the next 5ft. from this one, and the following and last seat ditto. Each of these seats will be 9in. wide, so that an extra rib, as before mentioned, must be here placed, as is shown in Fig. 31. In this *a a* are the ribs, and *e* a brace extending from rib to rib to rest the seat on; but as this in itself is not sufficient, two hard wood elbows are nailed to the seat at each end and on each side, which are again securely fastened to the ribs as shown. By this arrangement great strength is added to the boat, as the seat holds it together when under such a strain as might tend to expand it; while in the event of its getting crushed, the seat makes a good brace. The longitudinal stringers, *a b c* in Figs. 29 and 30, must now be put in. Of these *b* and *c* extend the whole length of the boat, but *a* oftener does not go farther than the floor.

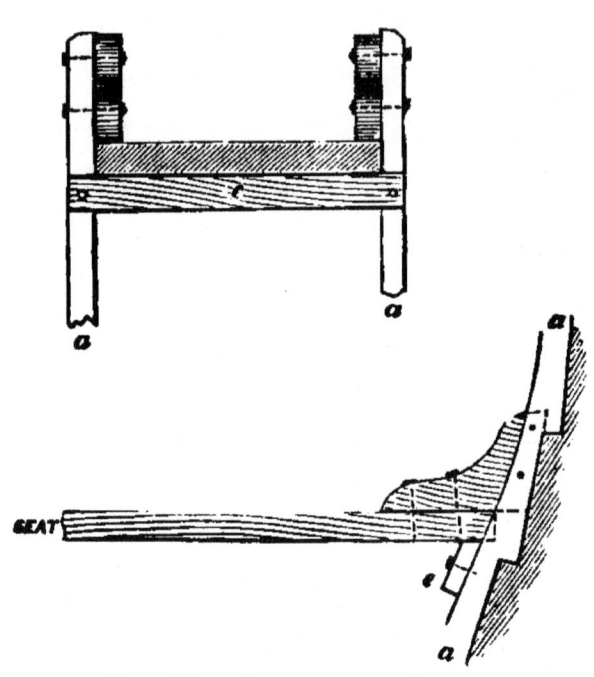

FIG. 31. FIXING THE POINTS.

These having been put in, the stretchers are now fixed, the arrangement for which is shown in Fig. 32, and will be easily understood from this. The stretcher itself must be made of ash, about $\tfrac{1}{2}$in. by $4\tfrac{1}{2}$in. is best.

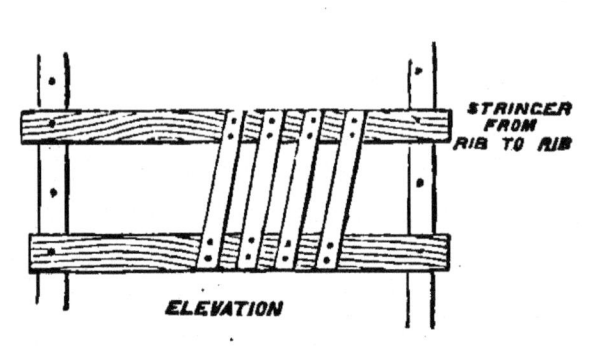

FIG. 32. STRETCHER GUIDES.

The seats in the stern must now be put in, the size of these varying according to the fancy of the designer. This must be secured as in Fig. 31. For a skiff of this size a plain seat, extending across the boat, is best provided with a back, and made rather broad. This must not be put in the extreme end of the boat, but placed 3ft. from it, and the space thus left vacant made into a locker. This is a very handy arrangement, and comes in very usefully if the boat is used for camping out, &c. Fig. 33 illustrates this arrangement. The locker is constructed by decking in the end similar to the end of the punt as described in Chapter III., and by putting from it to the under side of the seat wooden knees, as is shown by the dotted lines, it may be utilized for giving to the seat extra firmness.

The floors, which consist of pieces of 1in. material nailed across the boat, and resting on the keel and short stringers from rib to rib for the footboards to bear upon, must now be put in. One between the front seat and the bows, and also one between each seat except the last, will answer very well, and one under each seat as well.

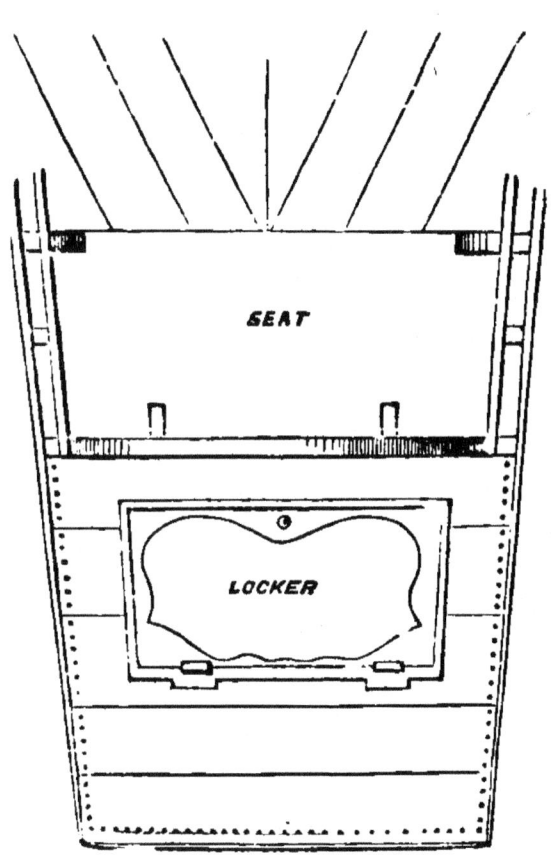

Fig. 33. Arrangement of Stern of Skiff.

Between the last pair there must be two. The foot boards may be made of ¾in. pine, and should be laid diagonally, as is shown in Fig. 33. They must be braced firmly together, and securely nailed to a light frame, composed of ¾in. by ¼in. strip. On this account they must be made in at least three portions—one to go between the last two seats, one between the middle seat, and one to extend from between the two front seats to the space in front by the bow of the skiff. Small recesses must be cut in the floors for the frame of the foot boards to lie in, which will keep all steady when the boat sways on one side.

A breast hook must now be put in the bow of oak and through fastened, as shown. In Fig. 34 *b b* are the arms of the hard wood breast hook. This breast hook rests on the top of the inside stringers *e e*, and butts against the back of the stem; *e* is the iron band rounding the nose of the stem; *d d* are ribs; *f f* are the outside stringer or gunwale strake; and *g g* is the skin of the boat. The iron band *e* must be carried round the keel, and secured about every 18in. with screws, but at the rounding of the fore foot at every 6in. This band may be of half-round iron bar, about three-sixteenths of an inch by $\frac{1}{2}$in. wide.

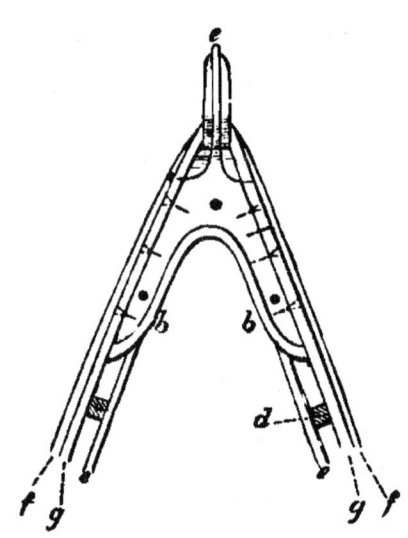

FIG. 34. BREAST HOOK OF SKIFF.

The rudder-pins must now be riveted on, and the rowlocks put in; both of these may be bought ready made.

The rudder and yoke must be made of hard wood, Fig. 35 giving the dimensions for this skiff.

With the exception of the varnishing or painting, everything is now complete. Nothing but good copal boat varnish should be used for a skiff that is intended to look well; painted boats never have the same finished appearance. It will be necessary to give at least two coats of varnish inside and out, allowing ample time for each to thoroughly dry before laying on the next.

If economy is not an object give it three coats outside. If the gunwale strake and the locker deck have been put in darker wood than the rest of the boat, a narrow cobalt blue band may be painted round them a little from the edge, greatly improving the appearance of the skiff.

This completes the skiff, with the exception of the oars and boat-hook. The oars are best made of larch or red pine, and must be 10ft. 6in. long over all. To make them well, the amateur will want some flat gouges and round soled planes.

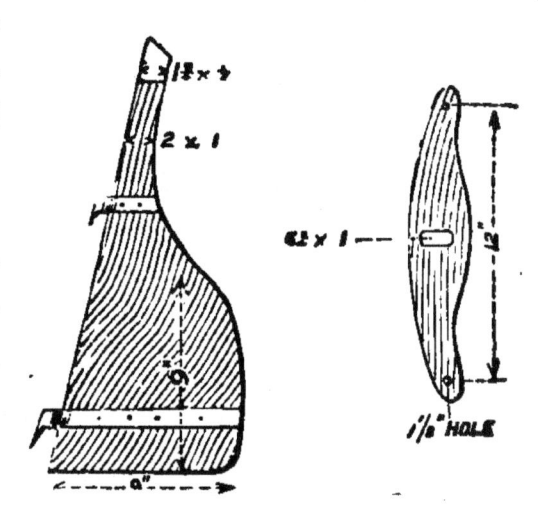

FIG. 35. RUDDER AND YOKE OF SKIFF.

The blades must be 4½in. wide at the ends, and narrow to 3in., and be about ⅜in. or ¼in. thick. The length of the blade is 24in. The neck, or that part just above the blade, must be oval, 1½in. by 1¾in., and it should be carried down into the blade, gradually dying out. From the neck it gradually swells to 2¾in. diameter by the grip, which should be 6in. long and 1¼in. diameter at the tip. A piece of leather 9in. wide must be wrapped round it and tacked neatly on with small copper tacks, at about 18in. from the tip of the grip. The end of the oar must be banded with a 1in. band of copper, neatly tacked. Now paint the blade and varnish them all over, and they are finished.

ANOTHER MODE OF BUILDING.

Boats are sometimes built upside down, or have to be turned upside down, to put on the bottom plank. For this purpose get a deal 6in. deep, by 2in. thick, by 30ft. long. Place under this transversely three trestles, one in the centre, and one about five feet from each end, the plank standing up on edge. Nail blocks of wood to the trestles, one on each side of the plank, as shown in Fig. 36, and secure the planks tight and firm, by driving a wedge if necessary between the blocks and itself, as shown in A, Fig. 36. The object of wedging it instead of nailing it is that the trestle can be moved up or down if wanted. Then, with such tools as hammer, mallet, jack, and smoothing, and rebate plane if possible, panel and compass saw, ½in. and 1in. finer chisels, tenon saw, spokeshave, fine bradawl, draw knife, and axe, the amateur may proceed to build his skiff.

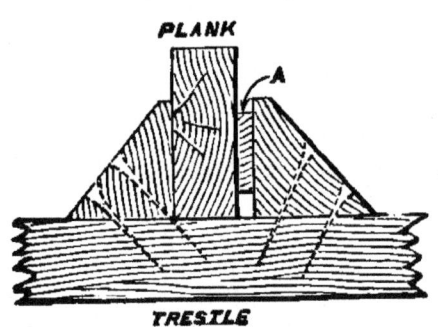

Fig. 36. Horse for Skiff Building.

The first thing to make is the keel, and, as there are two ways of making a keel, either may be adopted.

In the first plan—that shown in Fig. 19—the keel is cut out of the solid, and for a boat of this size it would require a plank 3½in. by 5in. square and 29ft. or 30ft. long. In the second plan—that shown in Fig. 20—two pieces of plank are required and some 2in. stout iron screws. One plank must be ¾in. thick, 3½in. wide, by 28ft. long, and the other 2in. thick by 3in. wide, by 30ft. long. Both these figures being drawn to scale, ¼in. to 1in., the amateur can get the comparative proportions from either of them. The design of keel shown in Fig. 19 is seldom used except for very small boats, as the labour of dressing it to shape and waste of material are very great; but when it is finished it makes a capital keel, especially in small boats like canoes. The keel shown in Fig. 20 is much easier to make; but in small boats, where the parts are small, it gives more trouble than the other plan, and is not so strong. This plan is always used in large boats, and is sometimes further strengthened with an additional piece bolted on the top of all. Keels made on this plan have very frequently a variety of woods used in their construction, elm and oak, for instance, being a frequent combination, as elm is a better material for holding nails than oak.

Having decided to construct his keel on one of the plans described, the amateur must cut his wood to about the right length, which in this must be about 27ft. 6in. This, if on the solid keel principle, must be roughly dressed to shape with the bench awl, but if on the built up plan, it need not be touched except to give it the right camber or rocker (curve), as the case may be. The surface thus dressed up must be planed quite smooth and the top piece screwed firmly on. The cambered keel means that the keel curves upwards. This will be better understood by explaining that, if the keel were laid on the floor of the workshop, the bow end and the stern ends would alone touch it, the middle or midships portion being raised off the floor, in this particular instance for 1in. The rockered keel curves downwards, or the reverse way to the cambered keel. The camber or rocker to the keel enables a boat to turn or answer her helm properly; if the keel were quite straight, she would be slow in doing so.

The next step is to get out the stem and stern posts and fit them to the keel, as already described (page 52).

The whole frame of stem, keel, and stern posts must be taken and fastened upside down to the plank which is fixed on to the three trestles or horses before described. This may be done in two or three ways, but the firmest and nicest way is to mortise the ends of the stem and stern posts, which must have been left

F 2

68 *PRACTICAL BOAT BUILDING.*

a few inches long for this purpose, roughly into the plank. If this cannot be done, they may be bolted through into the sides of

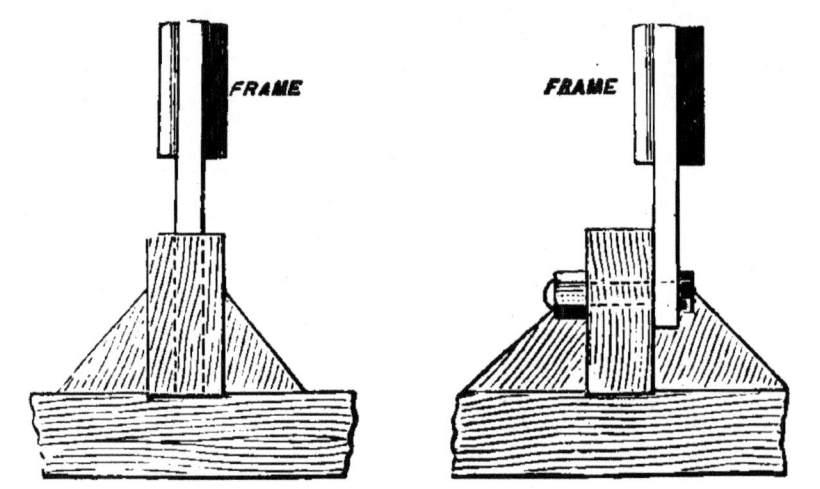

FIG. 37. STERN POST MORTISED TO TRESTLE.   FIG. 38. STERN POST BOLTED TO TRESTLE.

the plank, or they may be wedged in. Figures 37, 38, and 39 show these modes of securing it in its place, and which-

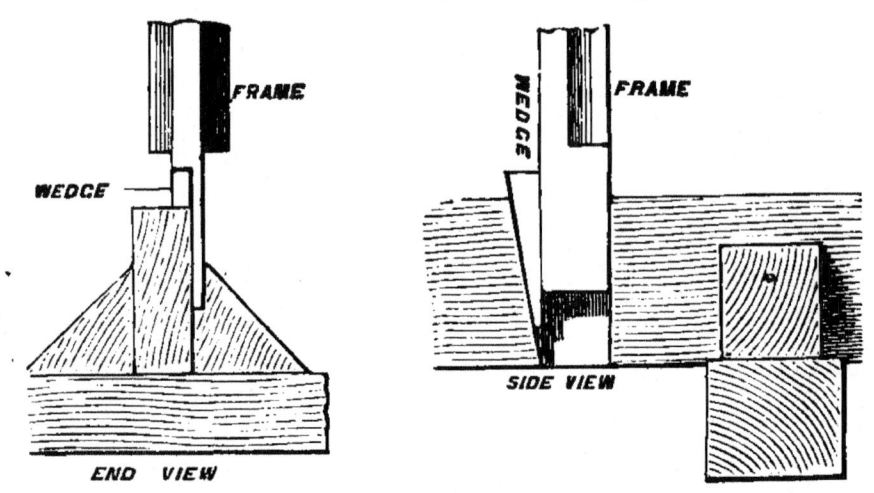

FIG. 39. STERN POST WEDGED TO TRESTLE.

ever way the amateur may select, the chief points of attention are to see that it is very steady and perpendicular. In all probability he will have to nail a stay on each side to the roof

CLENCH-BUILT SKIFFS. 69

of his shed, from the keel, to keep it quite firm when working on it.

Let him now from his drawings draw out on the floor or wall of his workshop a full size outline of the moulds, and with the outline as a guide, he must make his moulds for building his boat on, and to give it proper shape. Let him proceed to make them as described in Chapter III., and when they are complete he must fix them each one in its respective position on to the trestle plank and keel. If the moulds are made according to the lines shown in Fig. 40, the bow mould must be 8ft. 6in. from the nose of the stem, the midship mould 6ft. 6in. from it,

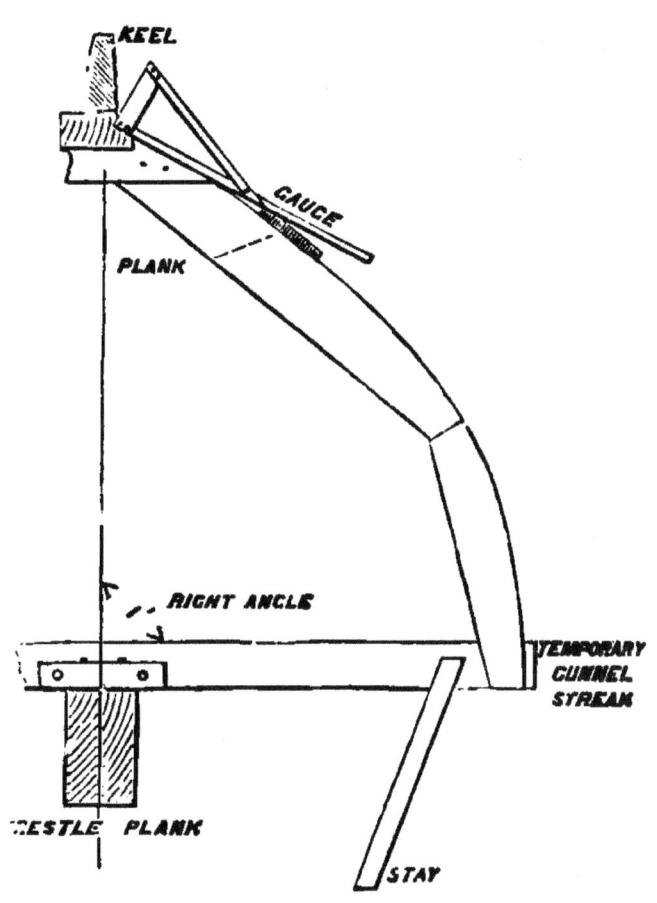

FIG. 40. GUIDE FOR REBATES ON KEEL, &C.

and the stern frame 22ft. These moulds must be put in very carefully, that is, exactly perpendicular to the keel, and quite square across the boat. If they are not quite true it will make the boat very faulty indeed. In all probability a stay will have to be nailed from the end of each frame to the ground to make it quite steady. A light strip of wood must now be fastened from the stem to the stern post just along the position that will be hereafter occupied by the gunwale streak. One of these must be put on each side of the boat. This will make everything stiff and steady.

The next step to take is to cut out and finish up the rabbets in the keel, stem and stern. For this a strong chisel and rabbet plane will be needed, and as some guide is necessary to be sure that there is a cut at the right angle a plank must be lightly and temporarily tacked on about two or three removes from the keel.

This will act as a guide, as in Fig. 40, which shows its action in a half section of the boat. On referring to this figure the amateur will notice that a light square is used; this is slid along the rabbet and the temporary plank, which gives the proper angle at which the rabbet must be cut. This portion of the work requires much care and judgment, especially when cutting in the groove at the bend of the fore foot and the upper end of the stem. At the stem a guide must be put in to act vertically, or the rabbet may be left in the rough till each plank requires to be put in, which will act as a guide to itself. This rabbet being nicely and smoothly finished on each side of the keel and stem, the stern post must be seen to.

Refer to Fig. 18, and from it make a full-sized outline of the stern of the skiff on the wall or floor of the workshop, and fit the transom as described. The next step will be the planking. Some builders put on the plank in two pieces, making a long scarf joint somewhere in its length. This plan gives far more work, but not such good work. Other builders saw out the planking in curves, so that each piece of planking is a portion of a large curve. How this curve is obtained has already been explained. If the planking is put on in pieces, an angle-box must be made to saw out the scarf joints with, so that each joint shall be true. This is made as follows: A stout piece of planking—say, 1½in. broad—is obtained, about 9in. or

CLENCH-BUILT SKIFFS.

12in. wide and 18in. long. Two more pieces, of the same length and about 2in. wider than any likely to be used in any boat, and about 1in. in thickness, are also got, and the whole nicely planed up on all sides. These two pieces are taken and firmly glued and screwed on edge along the length of the first mentioned piece. Little chocks of wood are glued on and against them, to make all firm and strong. These two pieces are set about 1in.

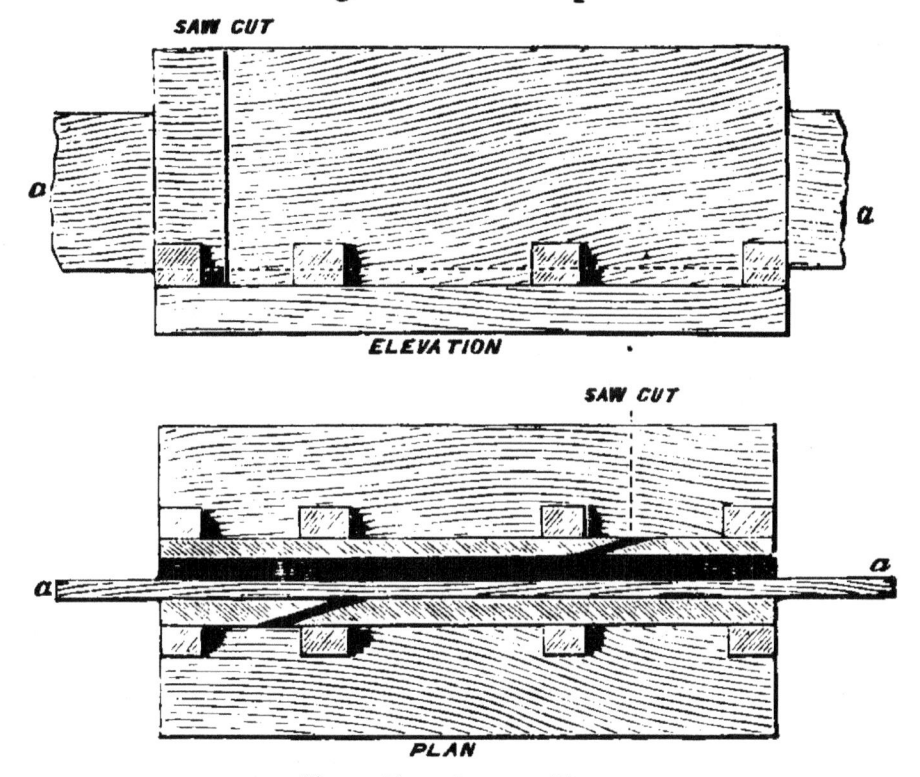

FIG. 41. ANGLE BOX.

apart and parallel to each other; down this groove a piece ½in. thick is glued. With a fine tenon saw a very neat cut is made at an angle across these. This cut must be very carefully made, and perfectly true and perpendicular to the bottom board. Great care must be taken to do this well, the cut extending down to the bottom of the upright pieces. The angle at which this cut must be made is about 10deg. to 15deg. with the slot which is formed by the two pieces. Fig. 41 is a plan and side elevation of this angle box. The way in which it is used is as follows: The plank to be joined is put into the groove standing on its edge, and if it is a thin one—say, $\frac{3}{8}$in. or $\frac{1}{2}$in. thick—a small wedge is dropped in behind it to keep it steady. It is then sawn through, the saw working down the cut in the blocks. As the angle of this cut with any plank that is put in is constant, any two of these planks will form a true joint with each other. In Fig. 41 the plank to be sawn is plainly shown, and is indicated by the letters *a a*; while the dotted line in the elevation shows the piece of wood glued to the bottom of the groove. The object of this piece of wood is to give the saw a clearance off the base board. The figures are drawn to a scale of $\frac{1}{8}$in.

In the skiff here described let the planking, whatever may be its material, be $\frac{1}{2}$in. thick and $4\frac{1}{2}$in. wide. It will save much labour to get it all ready planed up on both sides. To lay it on let the amateur proceed as follows:—First get some copper boat nails, nails of No. 17 gauge and $1\frac{1}{4}$in. long, and providing himself with a bradawl, which is rather finer than the nails, and a light tack hammer, take a plank and tack it lightly into the midship frame with one tack in the centre, so that its edge lays home in the rebate. Now let him take one end of it and lay it along the frames, so that it shall leave about an equal space uncovered at both the stem and stern, as is shown in an exaggerated form in Fig. 42, in which the extreme ends of the boat, the bow, or stem and the stern are shown, broken off from the midship for the convenience of getting it into a small diagram. In this figure *a a* are the uncovered spaces left between the plank, *b b*, and the keel. The amateur must measure his space carefully, and cut off from a piece of planking a suitable piece to fill each of these up. They will be of a triangular shape, pointed at one end, and of the full width of the

CLENCH-BUILT SKIFFS.

board at the other. The amateur must then remove the board he just now tacked on, and nail each of these pieces carefully in its place, spacing the nails, which must be about 1¼in. long for ½in. stuff, but in length not less than twice the thickness of the planks in any case, about 2in. apart. If the rabbets are not nicely made, so that these planks do not lie close to the keel, but leave large gaps, pitch, prepared as described in the chapter on punt building, must be laid along the keel before nailing them on. Now, again take up the plank that was just now removed, and place it in the same position as before, fixing it with a tack in each of the frames. With a fine saw cut off the surplus

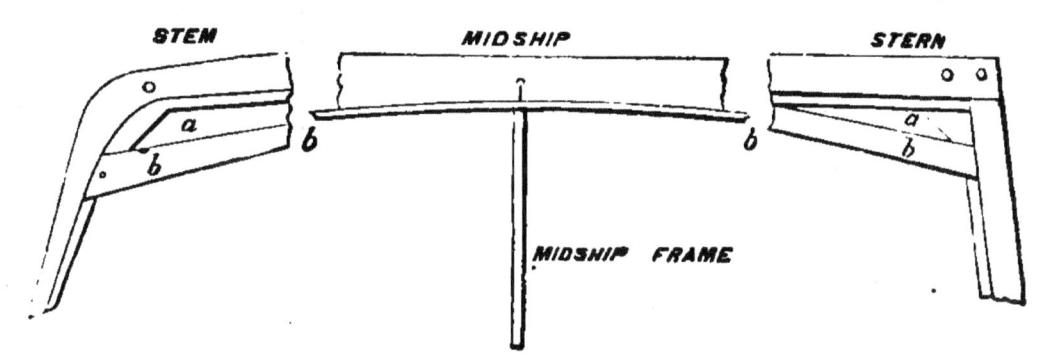

FIG. 42. LAYING THE FIRST PLANK.

material at each end to about the right length; do not cut it too short, and while holding it in position with one hand at the bow, with a pencil in the other mark a line on the upper side where the piece runs along that is already nailed on. Do this also at the stern. It will be found at that position where these pieces have just commenced that they overlap the depth of the rabbet in the keel, while towards the ends the overlap is very considerable. Dress all this surplus overlap off, leaving about a quantity equivalent to the width of the rabbet in the keel, which is three-quarters of an inch.

The edges of the succeeding planks will be bevelled as already described (page 58).

The best guide an amateur can have is to prepare a strip of planking nicely planed, and about 1½in. wide, which, with the assistance of some bradawls, he can fasten on to the frames, and extending from end to end of the boat one space or width of planking ahead of that which he is going to lay. Then on to his plane he can glue or screw a guide in the shape of a flat arm projecting from its side, and by always keeping this arm or guide in contact with the strip, which is temporarily pinned on with the bradawls, the plane will take off just the bevel required for the curved shape of the boat. The bevelling, for the sake of neatness at the bow, cannot be obtained by this means. In laying on the planking after the under planking is bevelled off, the plank that is about to be laid on must be planed down at the end to be attached to the bow for full one-third of its thickness; this is to allow of an easier manipulation of it. The plank being fully prepared must now be nailed to the one laid before it, the nails to be spaced about 4in. apart in the midships, gradually closing up to 2in. at the bow and stern. As the builder approaches these ends he must carefully cut off for the bow the plank to the right length, and bevel the end so that it lies snug in the rabbet of the stem: the fore foot always requires some care in this process. For the stern he must cut the transom so that the planks lay fair and square upon it, which having been ascertained, the surplus length may be cut off and the end secured. Till the transom is reached the stern ends will be treated in the same manner as the stem. The ribs must now be put in as described (page 59).

CHAPTER V.

THE ROB ROY CANOE.

IN this chapter it is proposed to show how to build a Rob Roy canoe, giving its dimensions and mentioning its peculiarities. Everyone knows that a canoe is only a modified boat reduced to its smallest dimensions, and it is, in fact, very much the same as the skiff just described to build, with the exception that it requires much more careful work, because, as it is small, the parts will not stand the same "dodging" in the event of an error being made.

There are many kinds of canoes made, though they are all on the same principle; some of them are intended for sailing purposes, and are, therefore, made so large, and have such a weight of ballast, that they are really boats in every respect, retaining a sort of fancied resemblance to the justly celebrated Rob Roy. The beauty of a canoe is its extreme simplicity and yet efficiency, so that when a great complexity is produced with sliding keels, topmasts, rudders, mizenmasts, &c., all the quality of this kind of boat disappears. Besides which, the portability of a canoe is, or should be, a leading feature, and not in any way to be despised.

Of the different kinds of canoes that have been brought out since the introduction of the Rob Roy, none have really surpassed it for general travel, though in special descriptions of travel there are some which are superior. For instance, the bluff lines of a Rob Roy make it a rather heavy craft to paddle against the current of a fairly swift stream, and so here a Ringleader has advantages; but the Ringleader is not nearly so handy as the Rob Roy on account of its great length—viz., 17ft. 6in., and some have been made as long as 22ft. For this reason it is not nearly so quickly turned, but it was claimed to stand rough water better, which, however, has never been really proved. The Nautilus, which is the other variety which is most adopted, is a decided improvement on the Ringleader, standing very rough water much better and is far more manageable, but it has the same disadvantage as the Rob Roy in being heavier to paddle. All these varieties have, in their turn, given birth to many others, and there are at least eleven distinct varieties of the original canoe, besides a great number of nondescript arrangements, used for fast or peculiar work, as racing and sporting. In a manual like this, where only a few pages can be devoted to one particular craft, it would be impossible to describe all the varieties; but for general work an ordinary Rob Roy is best.

A good Rob Roy should weigh from 50lb. to 60lb., and, by a careful selection of material, the amateur can be fairly sure of attaining this lightness. Of course, in canoe building the best materials alone should be used, and it is now generally admitted that oak most fully answers the requirement. Very good canoes may be built in cedar, teak, mahogany, and pine for the skin; but, except cedar and pine, they are not much used. If, however, the amateur is anxious to build a very light and strong canoe, and has the skill and the patience to work in thin material, there is no wood to be got in the English wood market that will excel teak. In selecting his material, let the amateur pick out good sound white oak, straight in the grain for the skin. This must be a bare quarter of an inch thick, so as to plane down to a good 3-16ths of an inch, and it must be $4\frac{1}{2}$in. wide. For the keel and stem and stern posts he will also want oak, and for the decking cedar (red) $\frac{1}{8}$in. thick. He will also require some thin spruce or red pine of a bare 3-8ths of an inch for floor boards and back board. Copper nails of 17 gauge and copal boat varnish must be used.

The chief dimensions of the canoe that is proposed for the amateur to build are as follows:

>Length over all, 12ft. 6in.
>Length on load-water line, 12ft.
>Beam on load-water line, which is also the greatest beam, 2ft. 2in.
>Beam at level of the gunwale, 2ft.
>Depth inside at midship, 9in.
>Depth inside at the ends, 12in.
>Camber, 1in.
>Distance of midship from the bows, 7ft. 1in.
>Proportion of length of beam of the fore section is as 6¼ is to 1.

Fig. 43 gives a sheer plan and plan of the canoe. In this the dotted line *a* shows the position of the midship frame in relation to the rest of the boat, and *c* and *b* of the bow and stern frames, which are respectively 3ft. 6in. and 2ft. 9in. from the midship frame. A shows the position of the hole in the stem for the tow-line, which must be ½in. in diameter, and B shows the socket for the mast. In the plan the dotted lines show the position of the beams to support the deck, while those in the sheer view show the position of the floor. The hatchway is 36in. long and 18in. wide.

It is hardly necessary to repeat in detail all the processes in building a canoe, because, as before explained, they are similar to that required for a skiff, therefore only the more complex portions will be described. The keel must be made of oak, cut out of the solid, as is shown in Fig. 19, Chapter IV., and its dimensions are as follows: For the wood, have in the rough a piece of oak 1½in. by 2⅜in., by 12ft. long; and the dimensions this has to be dressed to are: ¾in. outside keel, with a ½in. face, with a ¼in. semi-circular groove cut in it, as is shown in Fig. 44 at A, which is afterwards to receive the keel band, as shown.

78 *PRACTICAL BOAT BUILDING.*

The rabbets for the planking are ¼in. wide by 3-8ths of an inch deep. From this drawing and the dimensions the amateur will be

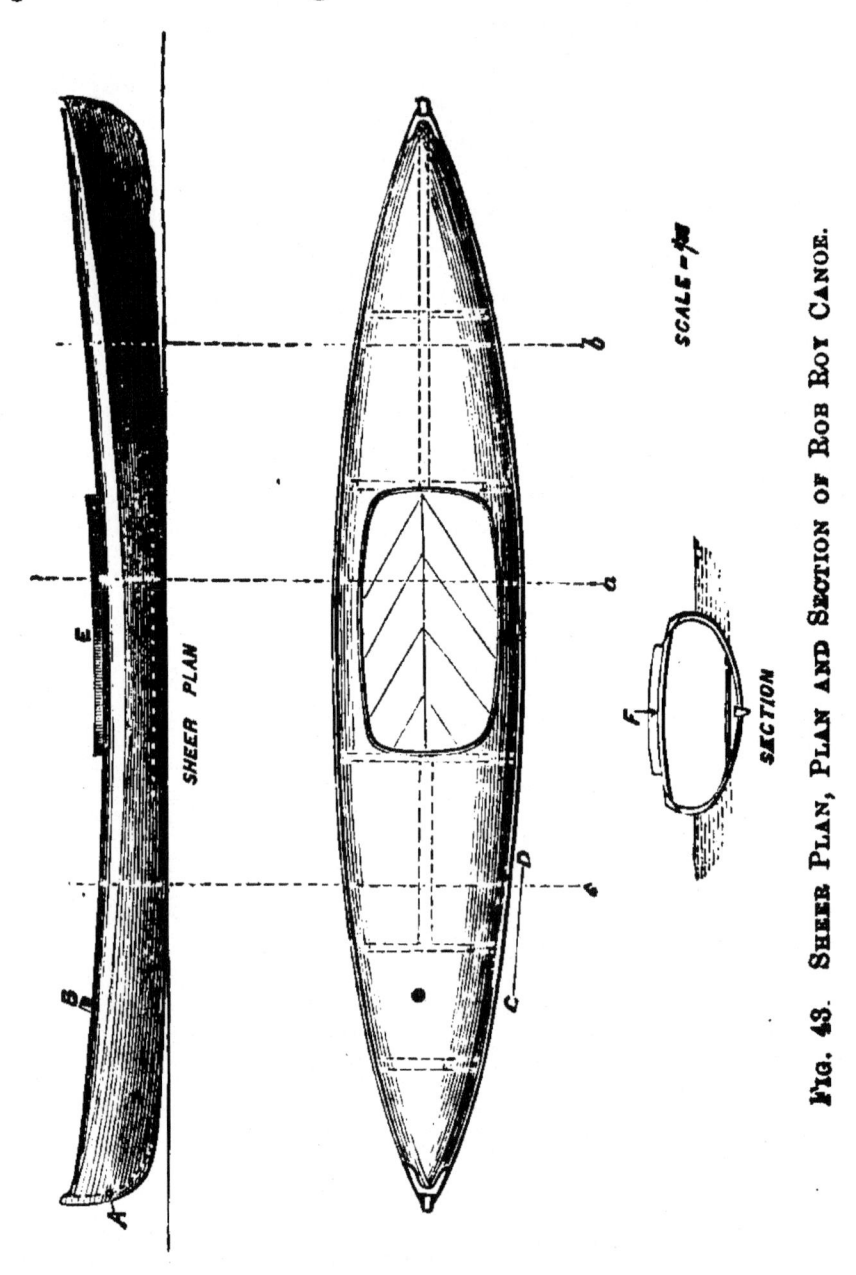

FIG. 48. SHEER PLAN, PLAN AND SECTION OF BOB BOY CANOE.

able to proportion the rest of the keel as in the skiff. In a small boat like this the amateur may vary his practice for fitting

ROB ROY CANOE.

the posts, and in Figs. 45 and 46 he will find two plans which answer very well but require nice work.

In Fig. 45 a wedge shaped joint, as at A, is cut in the posts.

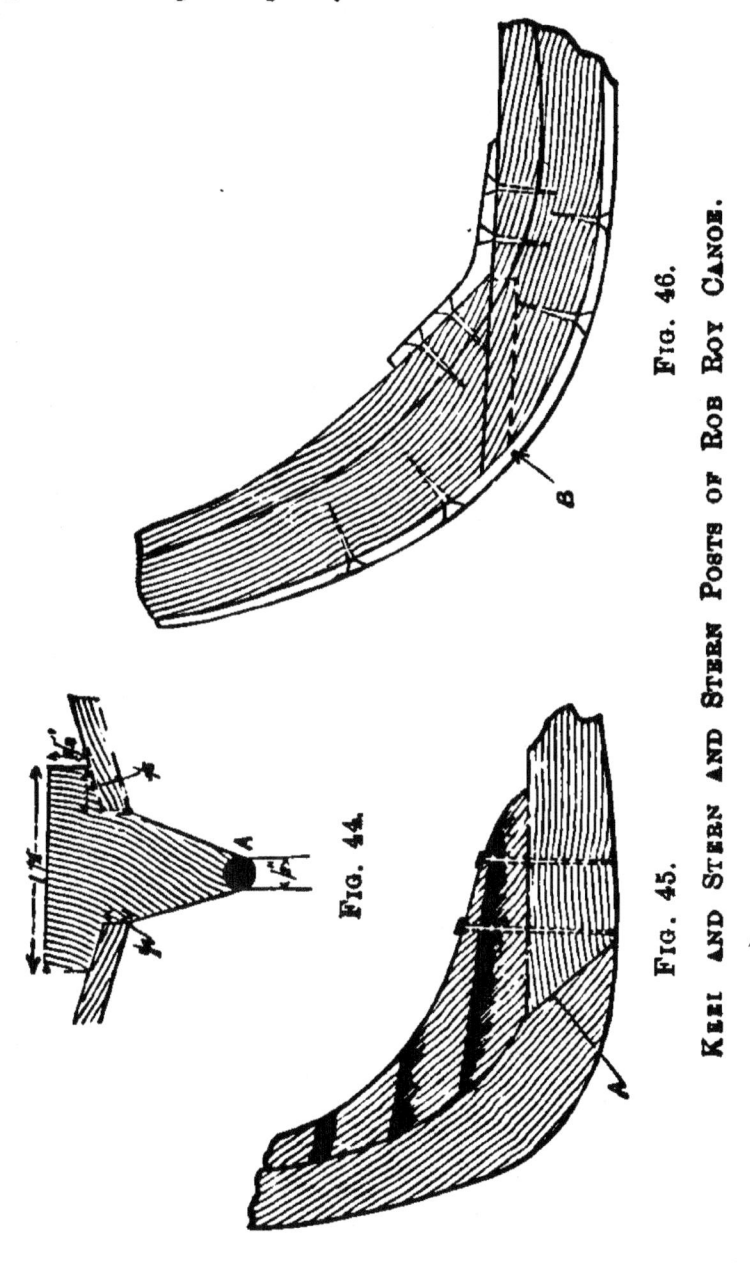

FIG. 44.

FIG. 45.

FIG. 46.

KEEL AND STERN AND STERN POSTS OF ROB ROY CANOE.

Two good screws, or three if the joints are very long, hold the posts in their places, the wedge preventing all rise of the posts on striking a stone. In Fig. 46 the keel is carried right forward, and the post lies on the top of it, as shown at B. Between the posts and the keel a small tenon is cut, which prevents all twisting movement of the post, while a small copper or galvanised angle iron at the back and the keel band, which in this case must be broad and flat, holds the post tight to the keel. The angle iron and keel band must, of course, be screwed on and not nailed. The fixing of these posts in a canoe is far more important than those of a skiff, because a skiff is not expected to get bumped about, but this is very often the regular order of things for a canoe, especially if its owner is fond of running rapids or navigating on shallow streams. For these reasons the bow or fore foot of a canoe should always be very well rounded, so that on striking a rock it may rise on to it and not ram it. Both the plans shown are very good for meeting strains caused by this class of work, that shown in Fig. 46 being well suited for canoes of great rise of fore foot.

The heel or foot of the stern post should be fitted just the same as the fore foot, unless it is put in square, in which case it may be fitted as shown in Fig. 23, page 54.

In a canoe the ribs may be similar in design to those in a skiff, but the dimensions must be smaller. In oak ribs cut out of the piece to shape—say, $\frac{5}{8}$in. by $\frac{3}{8}$in.—spaced every twelve inches with half ribs midway between; and for bent pine ribs—say, $\frac{1}{4}$in. thick by $\frac{5}{8}$in. wide—spaced every ten inches. A canoe may always have an extra rib or so spaced in about the swell of its length—as at C to D in the plan of Fig. 43—which helps it vastly in all work amongst rocky rivers.

The decks strengthen a canoe exceedingly—in fact, if it were not for the decks or some equivalent brace they could not stand the knocking about to which they are subjected. A more elastic material, like the cedar and birch bark of Canadian canoes, would be required. Supposing all the canoe built except the decking, and that the inside has received two good coats of varnish, the amateur must proceed to deck it. To do this he must put in the frames shown by the dotted lines in Fig. 43, and then dress out his cedar to shape. The frames mentioned must be nicely mortised in; it is the best way, though knees may be used. Having procured this cedar, which should be broad enough to cover in the half of the decking at its widest part, all dressed to shape, he must tack it down with copper tacks, spaced every half inch all along the gunwale and the frames to support the deck. The deck should be in not more than four pieces—one for the fore end, one ditto for the stern, and one for each side of the hatchway. This being finished, a strip of very thin clear-grained oak or ash must be obtained—1¼in. wide, 1½in. thick, and about 9ft. to 10ft. long. This must be bent round the inside edge of the hatchway, and nailed to the decking as a coaming, standing ¾in. above the deck, as is shown in E (Fig. 43.) It is not probable that the amateur can do this all in one piece, so he had better cut it in two, so as to get the joints on the centre line of the canoe on the highest portion of the deck, as at F (Fig. 43). The amateur will have to soften this piece, as was described in Chapter IV.

The amateur must now proceed to fit his canoe with the various iron plates, &c., necessary. The bow and stern should each have a nose of iron or copper, copper being that usually used, as in Fig. 34, p. 64. A flat plate of copper may also be advantageously used in each corner of the hatchway, holding the joints of the deck and the coaming together. Also two small brass cleets might be put on, one on each side of the hatchway, to secure the rigging cords to, and a brass socket for the mast must be screwed on.

Fig. 47 illustrates the sails and rigging, &c. In this A is the outline of the lugsail; this sail is made of wide cotton sheeting,

G

82   *PRACTICAL BOAT BUILDING.*

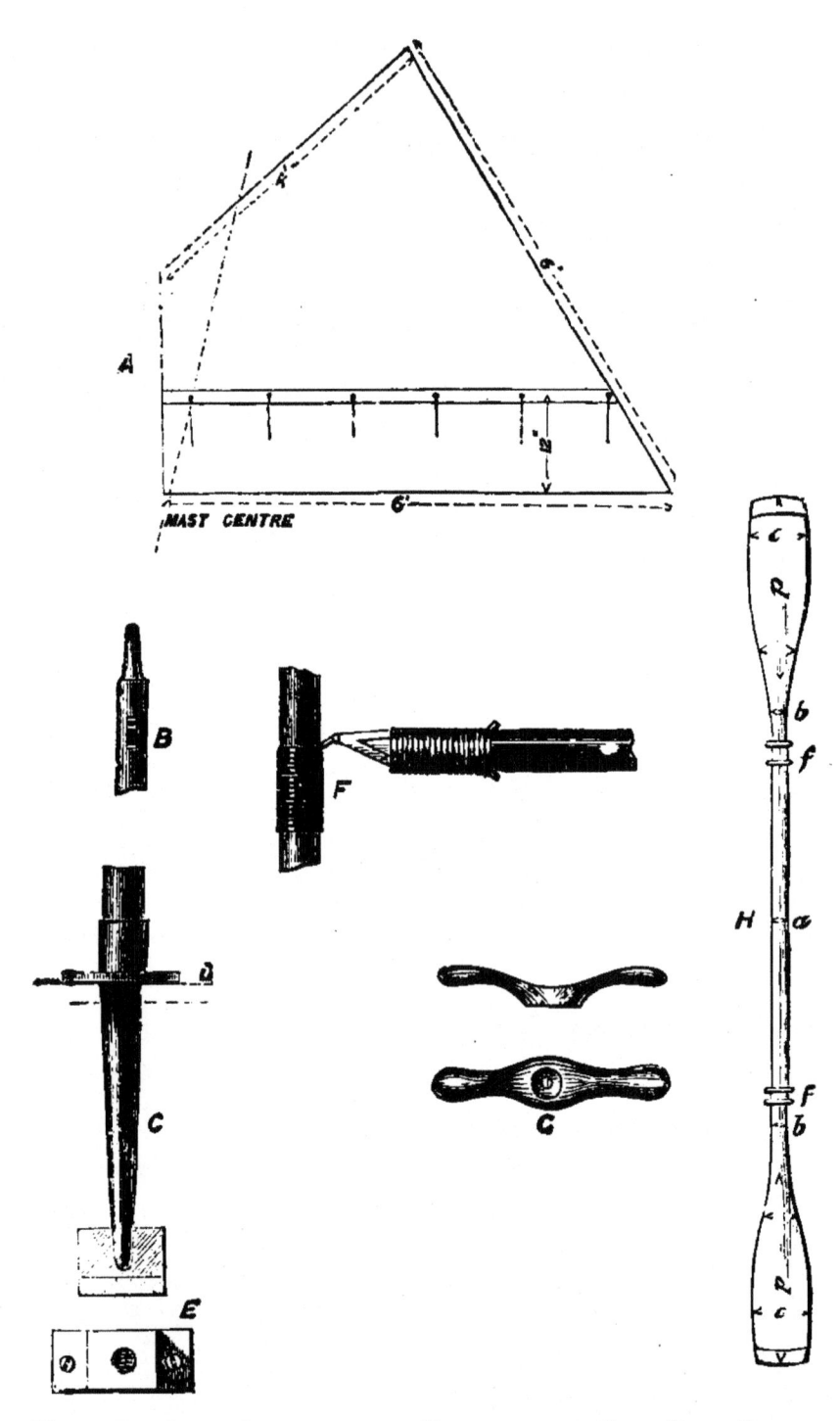

Fig. 47. Sail, Paddle, and Fittings of Rob Roy Canoe.

so that it is all in one piece, but round the edge is sewn stout cotton cord; and across, to hold the reefing lines on each side, sewn strong broad tape. No two canoeists have the same arrangement of sails; so this is only given as a guide to help the amateur to get the right proportions. In the matter of sails and cordage he will find nothing better than cotton for both. B shows the mast head, which is 1in. in diameter, and has a small blind pulley sheaf let into it. This arrangement answers better than a block. C shows the tail or foot of the mast between decks, and D the brass socket screwed to the deck, Where the mast enters the socket it is 2in. in diameter, tapering from the 1in. at the top to $\frac{3}{4}$in. at the foot. The taper should be very gradual, the mast being almost of the same diameter at 12in. from the socket as there, and then gradually tapering down to the pulley in a gentle curve. The total length of the mast is 5ft. 8in., and it should be made of ash or rock elm. E is a section and plan of the step for the foot of the mast, and should be made of a piece of oak, either nailed on to a flat piece, which in turn is screwed on to the keel, or else cut out of the block in one. F illustrates the attachment of the boom to the mast. This is made by taking a piece of strong soft leather, about 9in. long, and lashing it on with strong sail thread, or fine string, firmly and evenly to the mast and end of the boom, leaving about an inch of play between them. This answers every purpose, and is exceedingly simple and strong, and not liable to get out of order. The boom may be of 1in., tapering to $\frac{3}{4}$in., ash or rock elm, 6ft. 3in. long. G illustrates one of the cleets, which were mentioned as being screwed on to the decks, one on each side of the hatchway. H illustrates the paddle. This may be made of red pine or black birch. Its dimensions are as follow: Diameter at a, $1\frac{1}{4}$in.; ditto at $b\ b$, $\frac{3}{4}$in.; width at $c\ c$, 6in.; ditto at $e\ e$, 3in.; length at $d\ d$, 15in.; total length, 6ft. 6in.

The end is banded with copper, and there are on each end, at *f f*, two round indiarubber rings to catch the water that may drop down. The blades should be painted, and the whole paddle varnished.

In varnishing his work the amateur should allow as much time as possible between the time of putting on each coat, and especially the last, as the wood does not absorb the varnish so readily after receiving the first coat. It is also a point to put on the varnish as thin as possible. It is better and more satisfactory to put on an extra coat than to put one on thick, as the varnish dries much harder in the former case. When everything is finished, the outside of the canoe should receive two coats of varnish, and, when they are dry, all the canoe which is get-at-able should receive another, which is a final one, the canoe being quite finished when this is dry.

In this chapter on canoes but little mention has been made of dimensions, as it is impossible to enter into all the details that would be necessary to do so; but, as premised in the earlier portion of the subject, the amateur who undertakes to build a boat must have some knowledge of material and proportion. If, however, the amateur will take the proportions of the skiff, and reduce them by one-third, he will not be very far out. For nails, 1in. to 1½in. will do, except at the extreme ends, where 1½in. to 2in. are better.

CHAPTER VI.

THE SAILING BOAT.

Having described the punt, the skiff, and the canoe, a class of boats is now met with which contains the elements of all three, and that is the carvel-built sailing boat. These boats have the smooth skin of the punt and the shape of the skiff, while in design they in some ways very much resemble the canoe.

To decide upon what class of sailing boat is most suitable to the amateur boat-builder is a very difficult question, because it throws open a wide field of work. Of course, it must be a small boat, otherwise it would be out of the range of an amateur's workshop, and yet it must partake of the peculiarities of this class of vessel. A small boat suitable for fishing or shooting, yet capable of being rowed and sailed by one hand, would be the most useful craft an amateur could build, and a boat of this kind would not be expensive to construct. The following dimensions will make a very handy boat for either of the purposes named, and affords opportunity for the amateur to display his skill in designing. Beyond the outline of the plan to be pursued, with the details of the most complete parts, but little information can be given, but, if the amateur has carefully read the foregoing pages, he must be helpless indeed if he fails to get ahead.

Length, 15ft. over all.
Length on water line, 14ft., and 14ft. 9in. over the rudder.
Beam, 5ft.
Depth at bow and midships, 2ft. 3in.
Depth at stern, 2ft. 6in.
Midship frame from bow, 8ft. 9in.

86   *PRACTICAL BOAT BUILDING.*

In Fig. 48 is shown the sheer plan with sail set, and in Fig. 49

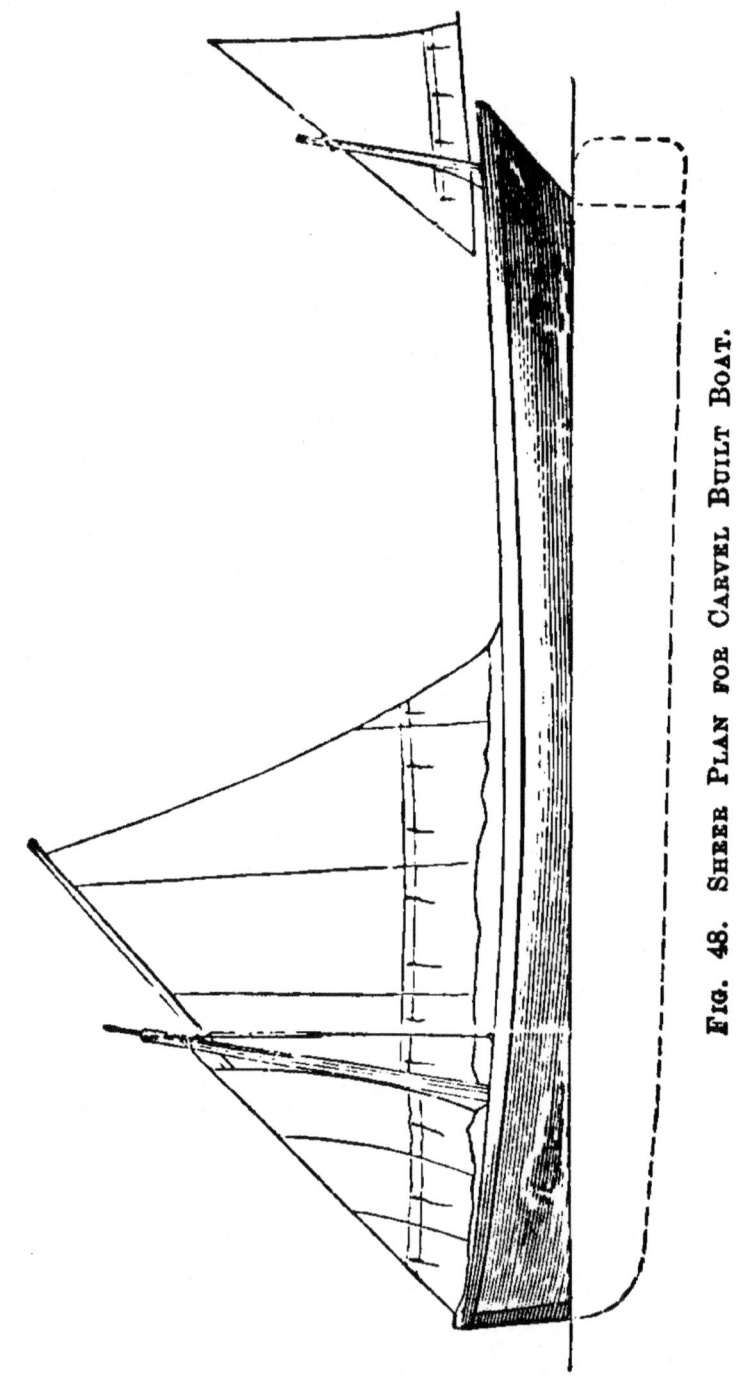

Fig. 48. Sheer Plan for Carvel Built Boat.

is the plan. From these it will be seen that the boat is half decked, the after portion being seated and floored. The first 6ft. is decked, then 12in. open, and then a seat for rowing. The next 3ft. 9in. is open, and then the stern seat. Beyond this the boat is open, and is very convenient for nets, cordage, anchor, or any other cumbersome article. The last foot of all is closed in, and makes a small locker. The amateur, however, will in all probability, alter these arrangements to suit his own ideas, and, as long as he does not destroy the harmony of the staying arrangements, it does not much matter.

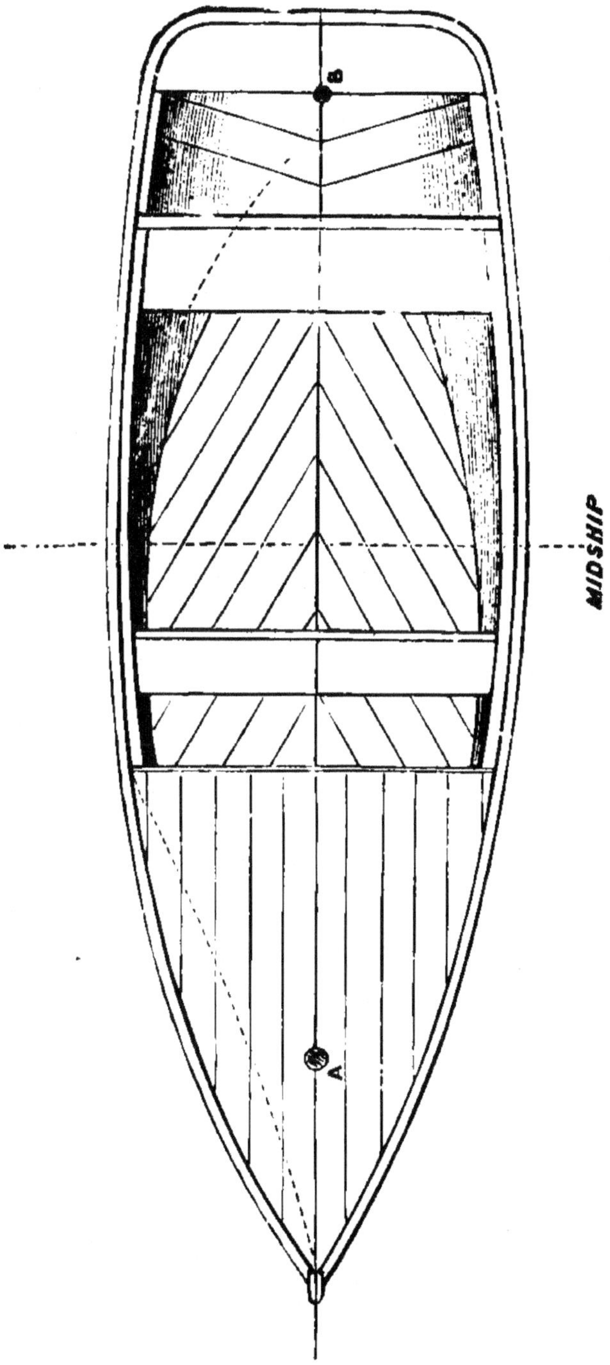

Now to proceed with the building arrangements. In the first place, the keel and stem and stern

FIG. 49. PLAN OF CARVEL BUILT BOAT.

posts must be made. Elm for keel, oak for stem and stern post. Let the stem be nearly at right angles to the keel, and stern post rake aft, about five to seven degrees. As the planking is of two skins in this boat, each of ½in. thick, all the dimensions for the rabbets in the keel and posts must be twice the sizes given in Fig. 19, and let the outside keel be 1¼in. deep. The knees for the forefoot and head should be bolted in, not nailed or screwed, trenails, however, being used in the tenons.

Though two skins will be put on, the rabbets made must be exactly the same as though they were intended for one layer of inch wood, except that in the stem and stern they will be quite level, and not "stepped." As there is a counter to the sailing boat, an addition, as is shown in Fig. 50, must be made.

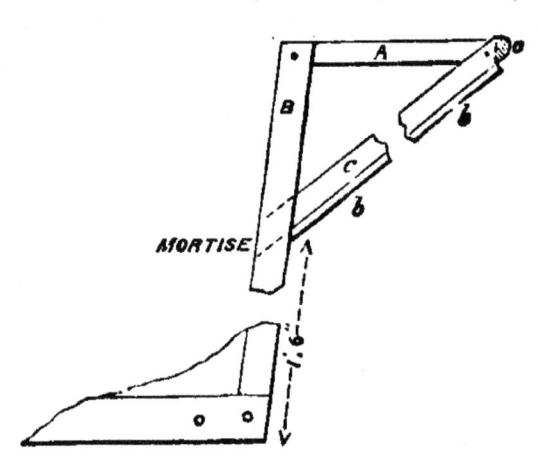

FIG. 50. THE COUNTER STAY, &c.

Each side of the stern post B, just above the rabbet in the tuck, a timber will be bolted, as shown by c, 1½in. thick, and 3in. deep, and again connected with the stern post by the carline A; but before the timber c is bolted on, a piece of ½in. plank must be fitted to the side of the stern post, to form the two sides of the rudder post trunk; another piece of plank fitted to the aft edges of the side pieces completes the trunk. a is a piece of wood worked to receive the ends of plank; b b a piece of wood worked over the stern timbers c, and also receives the ends of some of the planks in a rabbet, unless the plank ends are made to meet over the centre line of b b without a rabbet.

THE SAILING BOAT.

The frames on which the boat has to be built must now be made, and it must be remembered that in a boat of this kind these are not all temporary, but at least three must be permanent. The moulds may be built as described, but the permanent frames, or ribs, must be made of an odd number of pieces, such as 3, 5, or 7, so that there shall be no joint at the keel, but shall be evenly divided on each side of the keel. These pieces must be united with a scarf joint, as is shown in Fig. 51, and it will be best to cut each piece from the solid with a sweep saw, so as to have a thorough grain in it as much as possible. When they are all

FIG. 51. SCARF JOINTS FOR FRAMES.

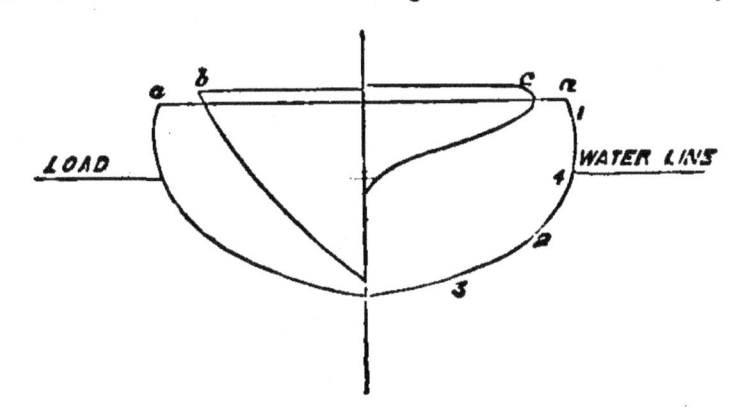

FIG. 52. FRAME SECTIONS OF CARVEL BUILT BOAT.

cut out let them be joined together and made complete, and then firmly bolted to the keel. These ribs must be 1½in. thick, by 2in. wide, or, if the boat is to be very strong, 2in. by 2½in. Fig. 52 gives the outline of the sections of the boat where these frames are to be placed—that is, one at the fore body, 4ft. 4½in. from the bow, the midship frame, and the stern frame. In this illustration, *a a* are the midship frames, 8ft. 9in. from the bow; *b* is the fore body frame; and *c* is the stern frame, which is just in front of and bolted to the stern posts. A temporary frame must be put in between *a* and *b* and *c* and *a*. All these being in their places, the inside gunwale streak, 1in. by 1½in., must be firmly put in and carried round to the end of the counter, and so also must be put the lower and upper strings. Copper nails and rooves of No. 11 or No. 8 gauge, and 3½in. long, for the gunwale, and 2in. long for the other stringers will be required. The fitting of these stringers is shown in Fig. 53, from which it will be noticed that the gunwale streak is only partially sunk, ½in., the thickness of one projecting. 1, 2, 3 in Fig. 52 are the positions of the stringers, and 4 is the position of the temporary one.

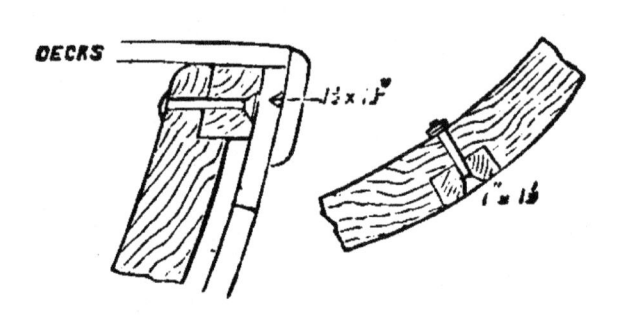

FIG. 53. THE STRINGERS.

The rabbets in the frame must now be all finished, as in the skiff.

The planking of a carvel-built boat is perfectly smooth, so quite a different plan of putting it on is necessary. In the boat under consideration let it be of red pine, half an inch thick; this should be obtained ready planed, to save labour. Now, before going any further, it is necessary for the amateur to construct the kiln described in Chapter I., which being completed, he is ready to proceed; but most likely he will find the assistance of another person necessary, as, without some experience, it is rather difficult to lay on the planking alone. There are two ways of laying on the planking of a carvel-built boat, the longitudinal and the diagonal plan; illustrations of these are given

THE SAILING BOAT.

at Figs. 54 and 55. In either case, where the curve is not great, the planking can be laid on without steaming by the help of a couple of iron screw clamps, as illustrated in Fig. 56. On referring to Fig. 54, which illustrates the longitudinal system, it will be noticed that the planks lay on to the frame and shape in the same way as in the clinker-built boats, except that the first skin is nailed on to the ribs and stringers only, but the second skin, which overlaps the joints of the first, is nailed on to it, so that they are united in one. The dotted lines show the joints of the under-skin. It is usual to put the planking on in three or four lengths, but in a small boat of this size a good deal of it may go on in one, but it may be necessary to use more on the curves. In Fig. 55 the diagonal plan is shown. Here the planking is laid in strakes, from the keel to the gunwale, at an angle. In laying on in this plan the planks are nailed to the stringers and ribs, as before, and the outer skin is nailed to the inner skin with a nail at each corner, where they cross each other, as shown,

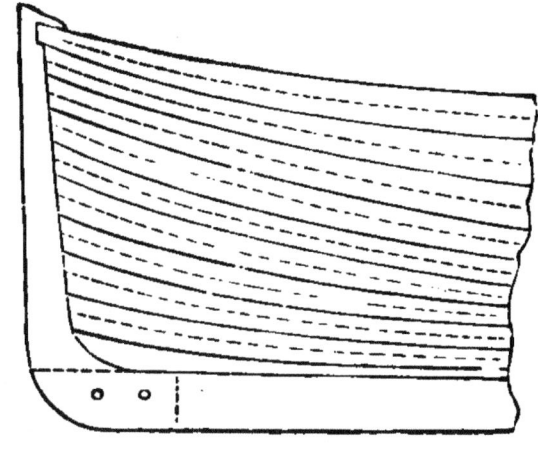

FIG. 54. LONGITUDINAL PLANKING.

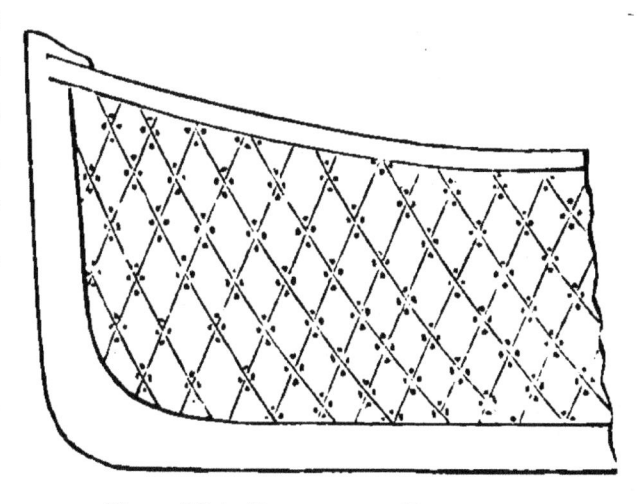

FIG. 55. DIAGONAL PLANKING.

so that four nails hold the planking together here. The planks in this system have to be reduced in width at the keel and gunwale, but at the bow this is hardly noticeable. The measurements are obtained in the same way as in the other, except that it is treated vertically. Sometimes boats are built on this system for the inner, and the longitudinal for the outer, because it makes a better surface in appearance than the diagonal; but the diagonal is the strongest, and, in very bluff boats, the easiest to lay. Between the two skins either a sheet of cotton or thick brown paper, well tarred, or luted with white lead, must be laid, so in the event of the first skin leaking, it does not go beyond. 1¼in. No. 15 copper nails and rooves are required for the skin.

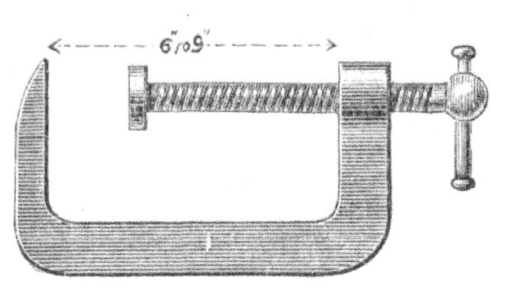

FIG. 56. SCREW CLAMP.

After the skin is put on, and all the nails rooved, the temporary frames come out, and the rest of the ribs and the floors put in; the floors may be of the same size as the permanent frames, and must be placed about every 30in. or 24in. side of the midship frame, and nailed through from the outside skin, with No. 8 or 11 nails, and rooved one on each side of the midships. The ribs must be made of 1½in. by 1in. larch or pine, and must be well steamed. These must be spaced, two between the bow and first frame, three between the first frame and midship, and four between the midship and stern. Short ribs of the same dimensions must be placed to support the seats, which will be put in similar to the plan shown in Fig. 31. All this must be nailed with No. 8 or 11 copper nails through from the outside, and rooved.

The decks may now be laid. For the fore deck, beams

must be put in to support it, two transverse and one longitudinal, above the centre. These may be 2in. by 1½in., the transverse being secured by braces to the hull. The ends of the deck planks must cover and rest on the inside gunwale strake and skin, as is shown by the dotted lines in Fig. 53. The decks must be of 1in. spruce, tongued and grooved.

When the decks are on, the whole hull must be caulked with pitch and oakum inside and out; but sometimes that portion of the skin about the load-water line is red-leaded instead, especially when the joints are very small. When this is done, the outside gunwale strake may be put on, not forgetting a stout ringbolt in the nose for the anchor. For the keel band ⅛in. iron is ample. The rudder must be made as in Fig. 35, except that it will have a tiller head and must be the full depth of the boat. For the oars iron crutches, as in the skiff, will be wanted. There are many other fittings which may be advantageously used, especially in the matter of rigging, but, as before-mentioned, the amateur builder is supposed to know something about a boat, and must, therefore, exercise his judgment in these. Supposing he has done so, the boat is then finished and is ready for painting, which must be done all over inside and out, using as little turpentine as possible in the paint. If he wishes to paint his decks, which makes them extra water-tight, and is a decided advantage if he makes a sort of cabin under them, he had better first cover them with a layer of unbleached duck, fastened with copper nails.

This will prove a capital boat, which will stand rough water; it should sail fairly well, and, with 3cwt. to 3½cwt. of ballast secured under the footboards, will be steady and safe. It is not too heavy to row, and may be easily managed by one man. For fishing and shooting on an estuary it will be found very handy.

94   *PRACTICAL BOAT BUILDING.*

Fig. 57 illustrates the sails, which must be made in canvas, sewn with proper seams, and roped round the edges. Unless the

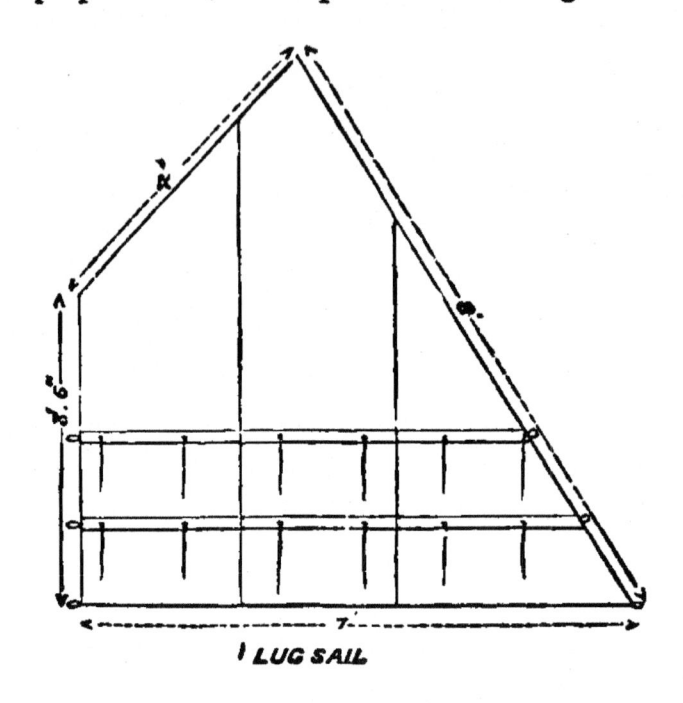

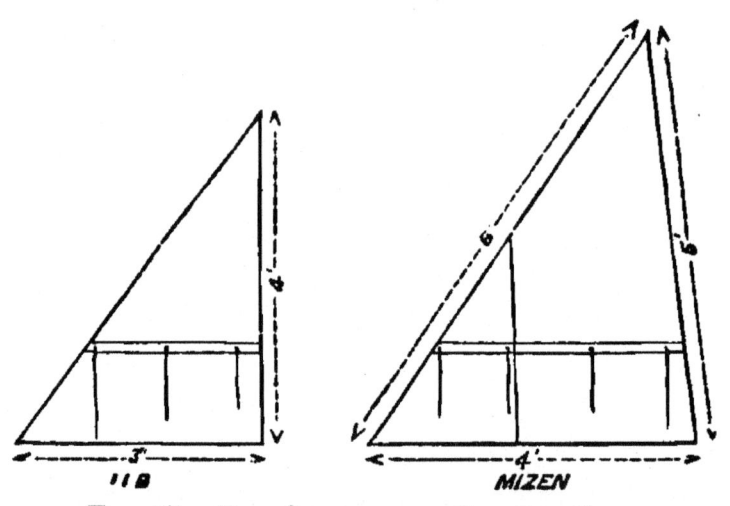

FIG. 57. THE SAILS FOR A SAILING BOAT.

amateur has had experience in this work he had better get it done for him. The mast stands 6ft. above the decks, and

THE SAILING BOAT.

is the same in shape as in Fig. 47; but it must have a block and not a sheaf let into it; in dimensions it may be 1¾in. at the top and 2½in. at the deck, and 2in. at the step. The mizenmast may be 3ft. 6in. above the deck. None of the sails except the mizen have a boom, and the yard of the lug may be 2in. diameter, tapering off a little towards the ends.

Space will not allow entering more fully into the details of this craft; the amateur must, therefore, bring his experience of boats to bear on the subject. Many pages might be filled without giving much more than an insight into it.

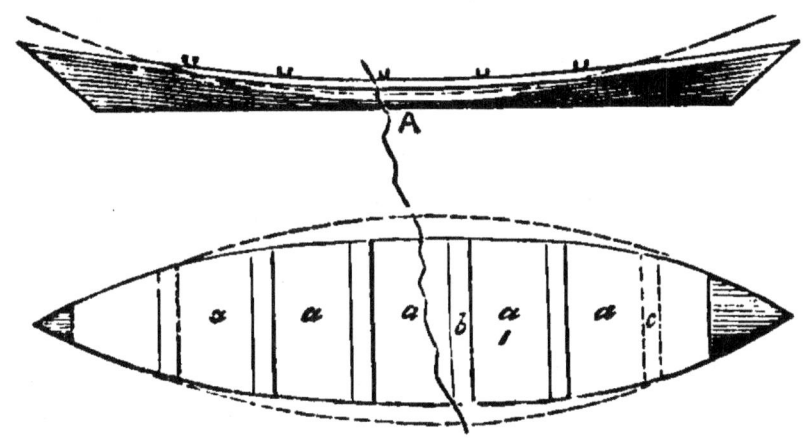

FIG. 58. FLAT-BOTTOM BATEAU.

Whether it is a clinker or a carvel built boat, there is so much detail, and this varies so much with the proportions of the boat to be built, that it is very difficult to give all necessary information at once. For instance, the simple fact of changing the mode of propelling a boat from oars or sails to steam alters the whole arrangement at once; and though an engine may be put into either one or the other, it is simply impossible, if they have been good before, that they can be equally good now. As this case is rather peculiar, we give a diagram to explain it (see Fig. 58.) The boat in question was a flat bottom bateau, 72ft. long, and rowed by eighteen men and a steersman. Its ordinary load was eighteen tons, consisting of pork and flour in bags and barrels. On account of the load being laid between the seats, in *a a a a a*, the men found it awkward to row, especially at *a* 1, where the bulk of the load was placed. At the suggestion of the boat builder, the seat *b* was moved and placed at *c*, two of the rowers being dispensed with, the steersman taking their place, except when in dangerous navigation and rapids. On the

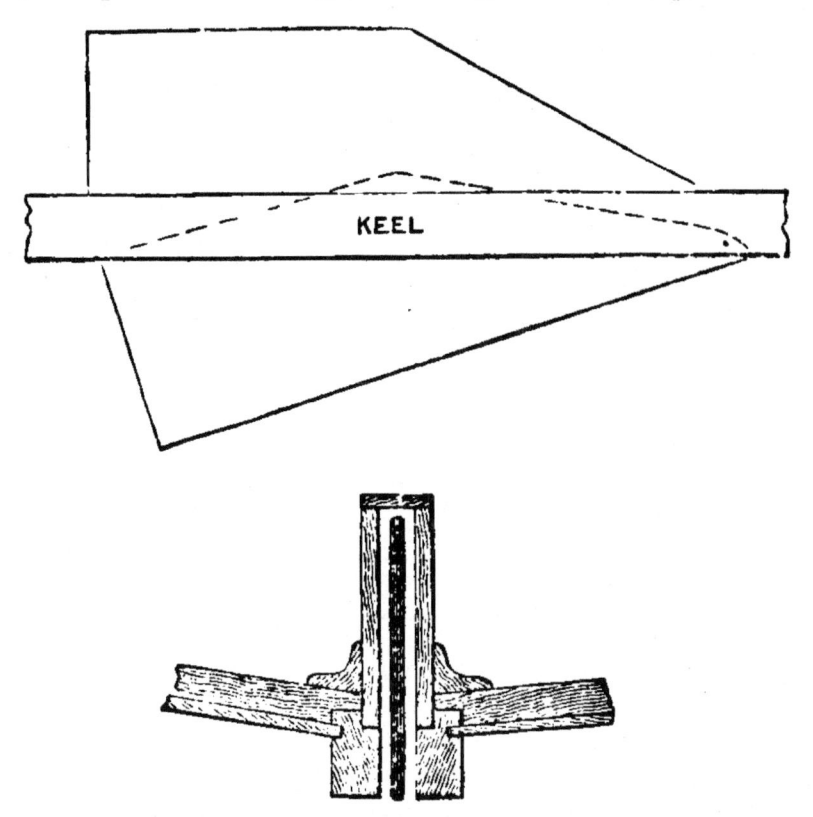

FIG. 59. CENTRE BOARD CASE.

very first occasion of loading up after the alteration, before full load was complete, about fifteen tons being on board, the boat collapsed, breaking at A. No doubt the seat had here acted as a tie, and held the parts together, so that the side planks formed a braced girder; but as soon as this was removed, it gave them the opportunity to "buckle," which they did, so the boat naturally broke in half.

THE SAILING BOAT.

For sailing, a centre board is generally found more convenient than a deep fixed keel. It is astonishing how little board will give a boat good weatherly qualities, and that represented by Fig. 59 (3ft. 6in. by 1ft.), would be ample for a sailing boat 15ft. long. The mode of construction is simple, and will be readily understood from the engraving. The "board" is usually $\frac{3}{8}$in. boiler plate. The sides of the case should be dowelled to the keel as well as side bolted at the ends. Of course the keel for a centre board boat would have to be thicker than the keel of an ordinary boat, as a slot has to be cut out of it as shown. The heels of the floors will be nailed to the top of the keel, and the case will be secured by small knees.

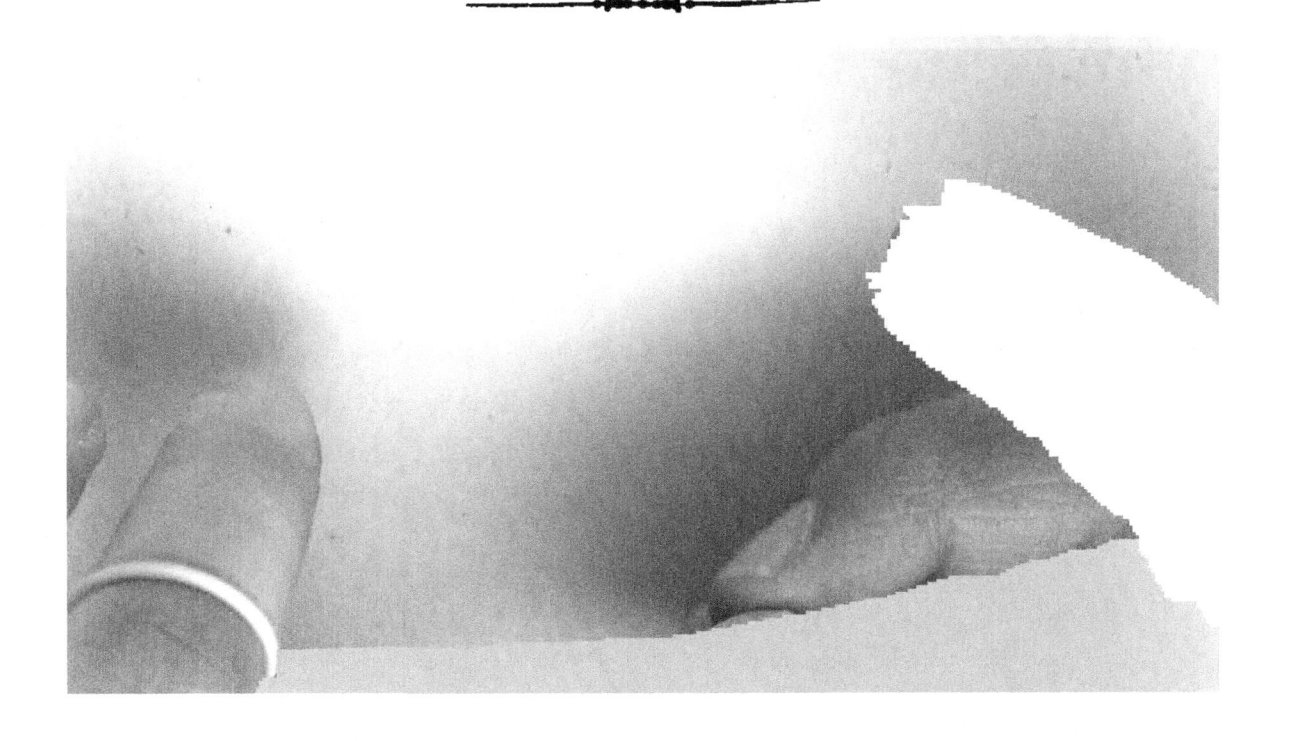

CHAPTER VII.

CANADIAN BATEAU—CANVAS CANOE—AMERICAN SHOOTING PUNT.

AN account of some of the more unusual and yet useful boats is often of great use to the amateur, especially as they are cheaply and easily built, as a rule. In this chapter it is proposed to give a very brief description of some of these, because from their general utility a knowledge of them is well worth having.

The first to which attention is invited is the Canadian *bateau*, a boat which is very largely used all through North America for every purpose—sport, commerce, and pleasure. They are made from 12ft. to 84ft. long, but the latter is an extreme size, 36ft., 45ft., and 52ft. being very usual lengths. They are easily built, being constructed very much the same as a punt, except that they are sharp nosed at bow and stern, and have a very great rise both in the floor and on the gunwale. Fig. 60 gives the plan and elevation of one, and Fig. 61 the section at midships on a large scale.

In the first place, to simplify matters, it may at once be stated that the same dimension of material is used throughout, that is, it is made either all of 1in. or $\frac{3}{4}$in. stuff, and if very small, say 9ft. or so in length, $\frac{1}{2}$in. is thick enough. There is one exception, and that is in the wedge shaped piece, to which the ends of the side planks are nailed, which is usually cut out of thicker make. Fig. 62 shows how this joint is made. No ironing is used in these boats, hard wood being used to protect it from

99

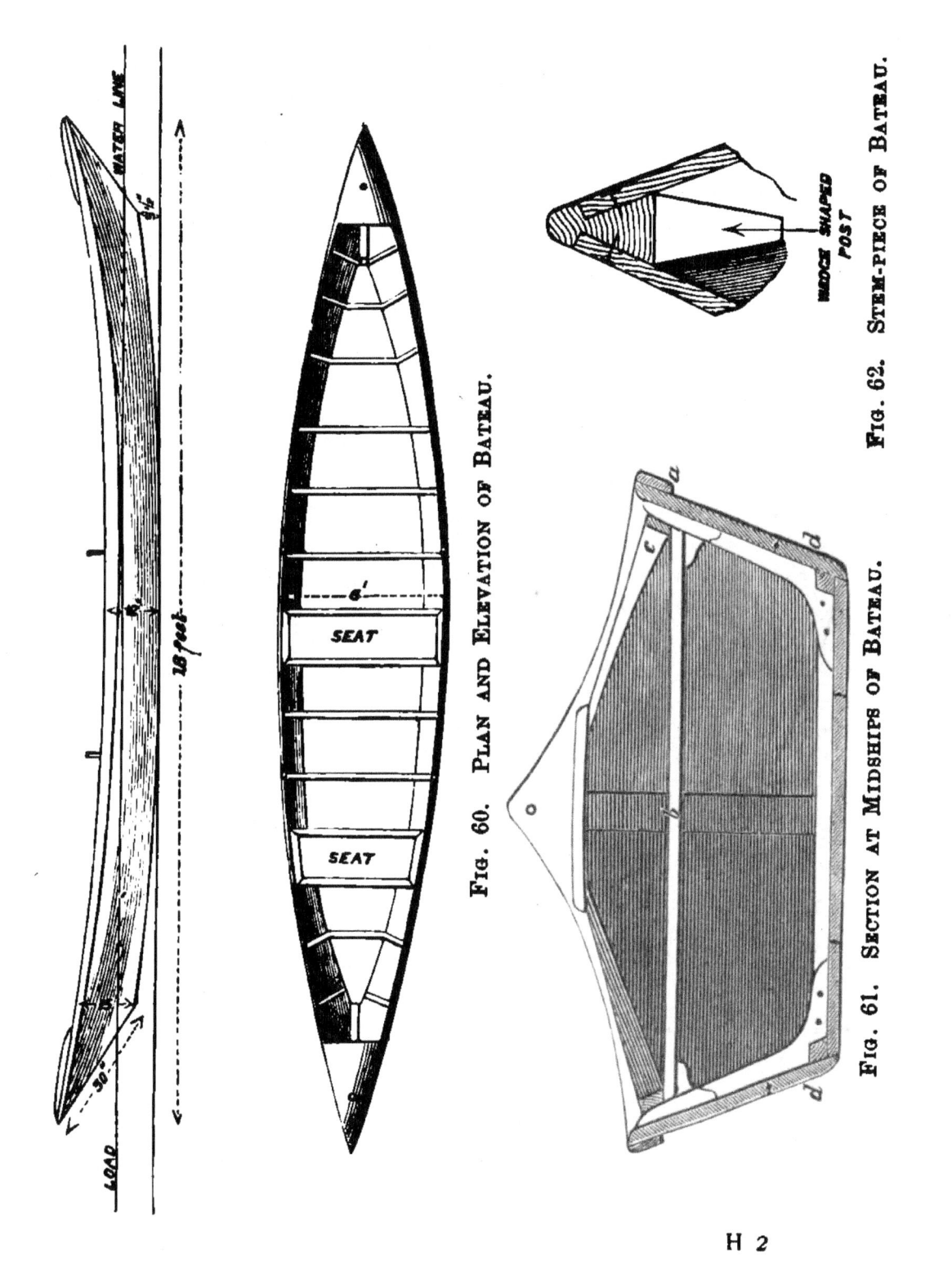

Fig. 60. Plan and Elevation of Bateau.

Fig. 61. Section at Midships of Bateau.

Fig. 62. Stem-piece of Bateau.

H 2

wear, and natural knees or forks cut from the woods to give it strength. Small boats are usually propelled with a single bladed paddle, and are exceedingly handy and manageable; larger boats are rowed and steered with a paddle, and under these conditions a Canadian boatman will run any rapid that it is possible for a canoe or boat to live through. As shooting boats they are exceedingly handy, as they are very steady, and draw little water, and in mud flats and marshes they may be wriggled over any ordinary banks with the help of a pole. In making them let the amateur follow the directions given for making a fishing punt, and using a little judgment for the bow and stern he will find a Canadian bateau the easier of the two to construct.

The next boat worth the amateur's attention is the canvas canoe, if it may be so called. A good well-made canvas canoe will, with a moderate amount of care and the exercise of a little ingenuity, last for a long time. It should be painted whenever it shows the grain of the canvas through the paint, and care must be taken to keep it dry; allowing drain water to accumulate in it soon rots out the canvas, for no paint, however good, can stand such treatment long. The following description is from a canoe which was built on the model of a Canadian birch bark canoe, and for handiness and practical use in the navigation of strange waters it cannot be surpassed. When once the canoeist has mastered the use of the paddle which is peculiar to it, he can do anything with it, and with two hands, one in the bow and the other in the stern, it may be taken down any rapid in Great Britain with perfect safety, the only stipulation being that there must not be any actual waterfall in the rapid greater than 2ft. Its dimensions are as follow: Length on water line, 10ft.; overall, 10ft. 6in.; beam on gunwale, 27in.; beam on water line, 30in.; depth at midship, 12in.; depth at ends, 15in.; camber, 1in.

CANVAS CANOE.

The load on a 6in. displacement is 387lb., and on a 9in. displacement 580lb. It may be safely used on a 10in. displacement on smooth dead water. The materials used in its construction are $\frac{3}{16}$in. by 1in. wide strips of rock elm for the stringers, and ditto $\frac{3}{4}$in. wide for the ribs. The bow and stem and keel are made of red pine, or larch would do, 1in. thick, and the outside keel of the same, $\frac{1}{2}$in. thick. The crossbars are also of pine, 1in. by 2in. For nails, $\frac{3}{8}$in. copper tacks are wanted for fastening on the canvas, except on the keel ends, where $\frac{3}{4}$in. are required; while $\frac{5}{8}$in. nails and rooves, No. 17, are required for the fixing of the ribs to the stringers, and 1$\frac{1}{4}$in. ditto for fixing the stringers to the ends, and also for the outside keel and gunwale streak. All these should be of copper. The canvas should be by choice No. 6 navy unbleached, but other canvas will do if it is close and strong. Some 1$\frac{1}{2}$in. screws are also wanted to fasten the keel and posts.

In constructing this canoe a frame should be built in the same manner as was described for the skiff, and the keel and stem and stern posts duly fixed in position as there described. Then the stringers should be put in and rooved and riveted. To do this properly at least three frames are wanted, and five would be better. Now turn the boat upside down, stretch and secure the canvas, and where from the shape of the canoe it will not lay properly, gather it up in a pleat and sew it down on the inside. The canvas must be all properly tacked along the keel with tacks 1in. apart, and along the gunwale at 1$\frac{1}{2}$in. apart. Then turn the canoe right side up and put in the ribs inside, bending them into position by sheer strength. These ribs must be spaced 6in. apart. Commence ribbing from the midship frame, putting one in alternately on each side. This is best done by nailing it first on to the tree and bending it into place, putting in a nail as it crosses each stringer from the outside. When all the ribs are done and the width of the parts where the crossbars come are known, take out the frame. Now put in the inside and the outside gunwale streak. See if all the canvas is tight; and, if so, put in an auxiliary rib at each place where the canvas is gathered, and tack the canvas to it. If it is not all quite tight put on some temporary crossbars, expanding or contracting the width of the canoe half an inch or so till it is. If it is still not quite tight it can be gathered up more till it is. It can be made quite tight in all cases. When it is got properly tight put on the cross bars, of which there are five, with brass screws, two in each end, and cover in the ends with canvas. Now turn the canoe upside down, and put on the outside keel, driving the nails right through, and clinching them, after having given the parts which will be covered by it a good coat of thick paint. The whole canoe inside

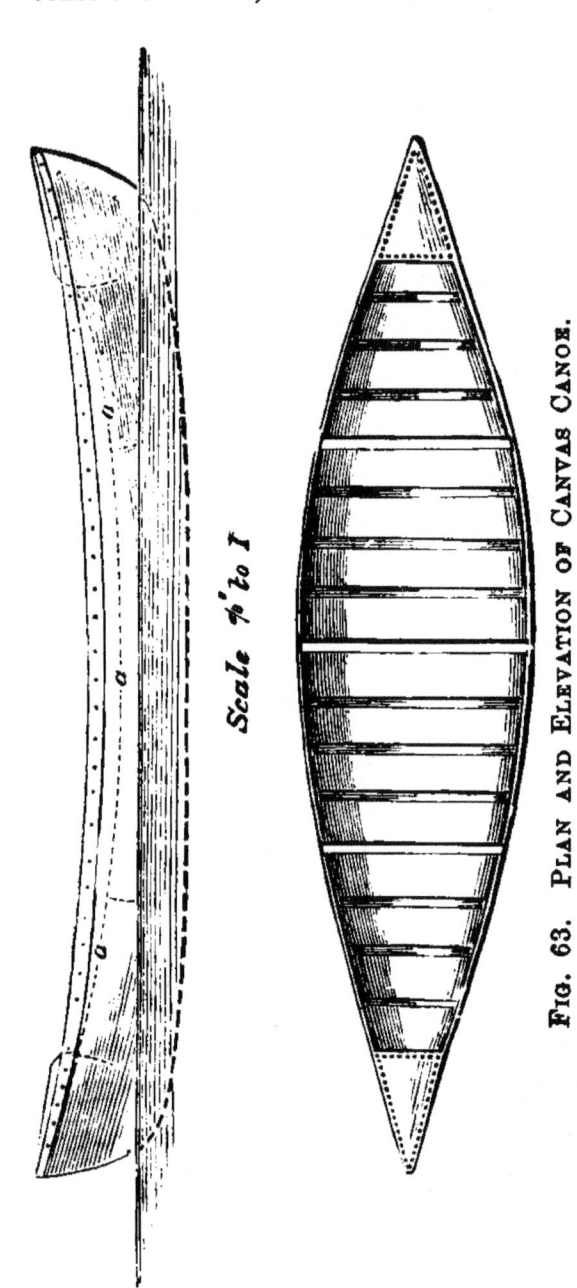

FIG. 63. PLAN AND ELEVATION OF CANVAS CANOE.

Scale ½ to 1

CANVAS CANOE. 103

and out may then receive three good coats of paint, and, when quite dry, one of copal boat varnish. If the entrance of the fore-foot and keel, and that portion of the gunwale strake when paddling, receive a nicely put on layer of sheet gutta percha, three-tenths of an inch thick, to prevent wear, so much the better. Vulcanised rubber is better than gutta percha, but harder to cement on. Fig. 63 illustrates this canoe in elevation and plan, and from this view and those given in Figs. 64, 65, 66,

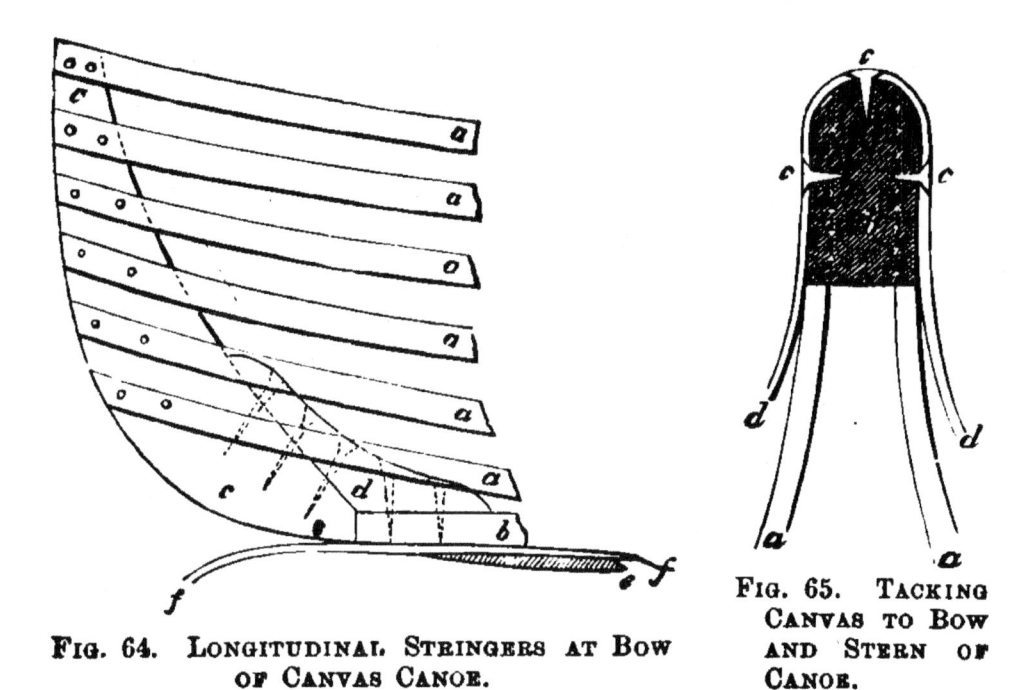

FIG. 64. LONGITUDINAL STRINGERS AT BOW OF CANVAS CANOE.

FIG. 65. TACKING CANVAS TO BOW AND STERN OF CANOE.

the amateur will be able to form a very fair idea of the craft. In Fig. 64 the position of the longitudinal stringers (*a a a a a a*) on the midship frame is given, and in Fig. 65 they are shown where fastened to stem post. In Fig. 63, in the plan, the positions of the ribs are shown as well as the five crossbars. The mode of tacking on the canvas to the bow and stern—the most troublesome places—is also shown in Fig. 65 (*a a*, the stringers; *b*, stem or stern post; *c*, tacks; *d*, canvas), while in the elevation of Fig. 63 the dotted lines show where the gathering in is necessary, but

104 PRACTICAL BOAT BUILDING.

the line *a a a* shows the position of the joint if only narrow canvas is used. One of the paddles by which it is propelled is

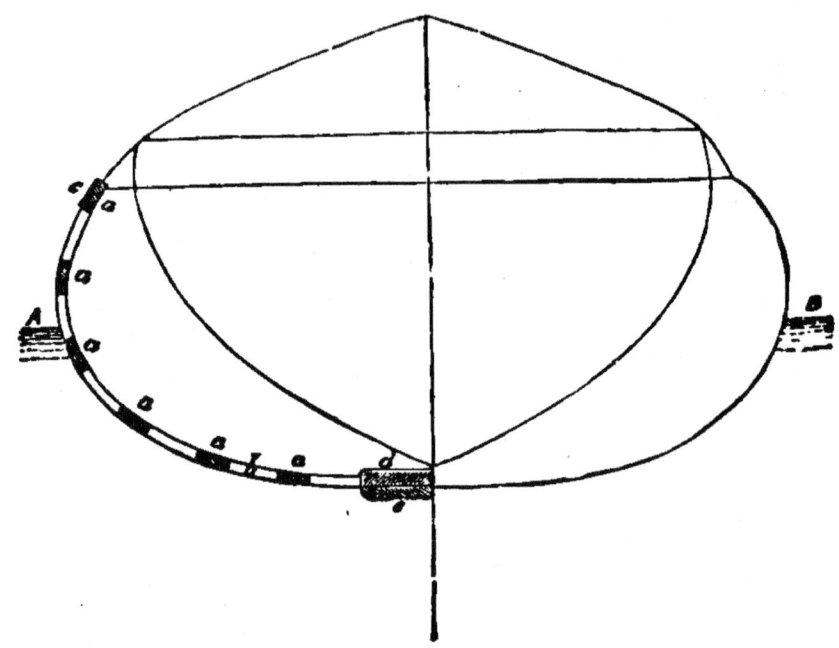

FIG. 66. CROSS SECTION OF CANVAS CANOE, SHOWING LONGITUDINAL STRINGERS.

shown in Fig. 67. Two of these paddles are required, one for the bow and one for the stern, the stern alone being used if there

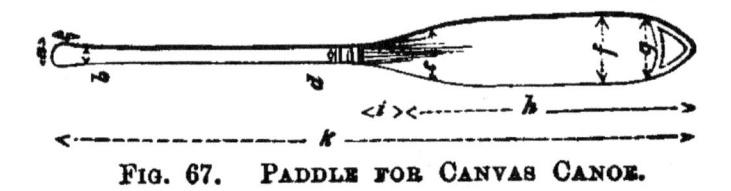

FIG. 67. PADDLE FOR CANVAS CANOE.

is only one occupant of the boat. The stern paddle is much larger than the bow paddle. The following table gives the dimensions of each:

Stern.	Bow.	Stern.	Bow.
a 1¼in.	1¼in.	*f* 6in.	5in.
b 1in.	1in.	*g* 4¼in.	4in.
c 2in.	2in.	*h* 24in.	24in.
d ¾in.	¾in.	*i* 4¼in.	4in.
e 4in.	4in.	*k* 4ft. 9in.	4ft.

SHOOTING PUNT.

The last boat I would draw attention to is the American canvas shooting punt, which for portability is perhaps unequalled. This punt is made of waterproof canvas stretched over a frame which is so constructed as to fold up into a very compact space. They are chiefly used for flats and marshes, and are therefore made to pole, though they can be rowed. In shape they are very similar to an ordinary English fishing punt, except that the sides flare out. In length they are generally from 12ft. to 15ft. by 3ft. wide, and 1ft. deep. Figs. 68, 69, and 70 illustrate one,

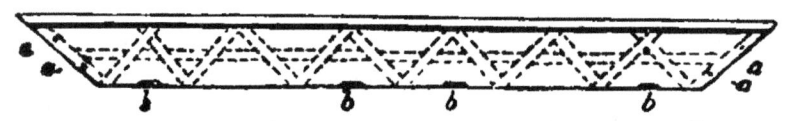

FIG. 68. ELEVATION OF AMERICAN SHOOTING PUNT.

and from these, with the exercise of a little ingenuity, the amateur should be able to make it. They are bolted together with 3-16ths of an inch brass bolts with winged nuts, the hinges

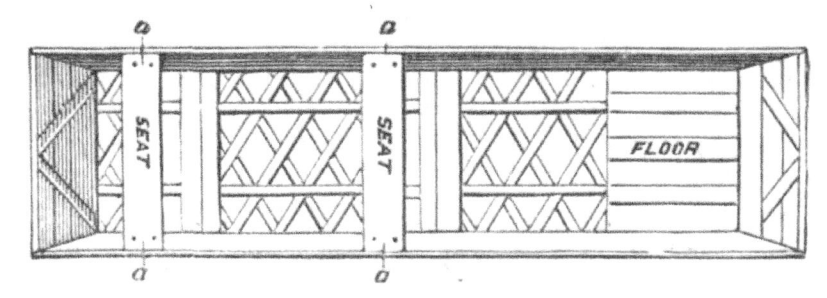

FIG. 69. PLAN OF AMERICAN SHOOTING PUNT.

used being ordinary bar cut hinges. Pine or rock elm is used for the frame, and indiarubber draft excluder is used to make the joints tight. Referring to these figures, $a\ a\ a\ a$ are winged bolts; $b\ b\ b\ b$, the position of the hinges; and $c\ c$, in Fig. 70, the loose canvas fold round the hinged joints. The frame of the boat is laid diagonally, and there is no floor proper except a small portion for the punter to stand on, and under each seat there is a narrow piece for the shooter's feet. The sides all fold in on the bottom, and the two seats are then bolted on to them in such a manner as to hold it all firm together for travelling. These punts are very light and portable, and easily opened out or closed, so that in shooting over uncertain ground they are very handy, as a man can close one up and carry it for a mile or more on his head without any great inconvenience or waste of time.

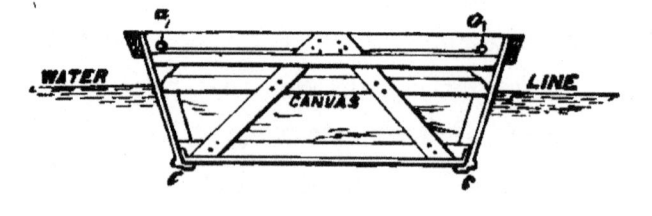

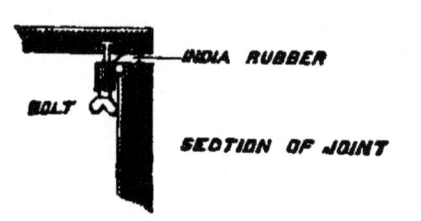

FIG. 70. CROSS SECTION AND JOINT OF AMERICAN SHOOTING PUNT.

INDEX.

A.
Anvil for boat building, 45
Angles for scarfs, 71
Area of load water line, 17

B.
Ballast, 93
Battens for drawing, 7
Bench and vice, 28
Bent timbers, 60
Bevelling, 58
Bilge planking, 57
Boat building upside down, 65
Books on yacht and boat designing, 6
Breast hooks, 64

C.
Canoes, 77
Canvas canoe, 100
Canadian bateau, 98
Caulking tools, 45
Centre board for sailing boat, 96
Centre of buoyancy, 15
    Gravity, 15
    Lateral resistance, 17
Clamp with screw, 92
Clamps for boat building, 57
Cleat for fixing plank, 56
Clench work, 49
Curves for drawing, 6
Co-efficient of displacement, 17

D.
Deck of sailing boat, 93
Designing a boat, 8
Displacement, to calculate, 17
Drawing instruments, 8
Drawing, laying off a, 23

E.
Experiment to find centre of buoyancy, 15
Experiment to find centre of lateral resistance, 16

F.
Fairing a drawing, 14
Fishing punt, 35
Floor timbers, 59
Fresh water, weight of, 17

G.
Garboard strake, 56
Gravity, centre of, 15
Gauge, 56
Gunwale strake, 55, 58, 61, 90

J.
Joggles, 60

INDEX.

K.
Keel, to lay, 51
Keel, stem and stern post, 53
Keels, forms of, 52, 96
Kiln for steaming, 25
Knees, 62, 88, 96

L.
Laying off a drawing, 23

M.
Materials for boat building, 28
Moulds for boat building, 23

N.
Nails for boat building, 33
Nautilus canoe, 5, 76

P.
Paint for boats, 34
Pear-shaped curves, 6
Pearl canoe, 5
Planking, 55
Punt, to build, 35

R.
Ribs, 59
Ringleader canoe, 5, 76
Rob Roy canoe, 75
    Dimensions of, 77
    Bevelling of, 77
    Sails, &c., 82
    Weight of, 76
Rooves for boat building, 33
Rudders, 64

S.
Sailing boat, designs for, 86
    Building one, 85
Sails for sailing boat, 94
    Rob Roy canoe, 82
Salt water, weight of, 17
Scarfs, 70
Shooting punt of America, 105
Skiff, building one, 49
    For rowing, 50
Spline battens, 7
Stanley, maker of drawing instruments, 8
Steam kiln, 25
Stem and stern post, 53
Stocks for boat building, 22
Stretcher guides, 62
Stringers, 61

T.
Timbers, fixing, 60
Tools used in boat building, 19
Top strake, 58
Transom, 55
Trestles for boat building, 22

V.
Varnish, 64

W.
Water, weight of, 17
Weights used in drawing, 7
Woods for boat building, 28

Printed in Great Britain
by Amazon